Developing
Listening
Skills
1

Developing **Listening** Skills Book **1**

Publisher   Chung Kyudo
Editors   Kim Jinsuk, Cho Sangik
Author   Michael A. Putlack
Designers   Yoon Jiyoung, Park Sunyoung

First published in December 2013
By Darakwon, Inc.
Darakwon Bldg., 211, Munbal-ro, Paju-si, Gyeonggi-do 10881
Republic of Korea
Tel: 82-2-736-2031 (Ext. 250)
Fax: 82-2-732-2037

ISBN   978-89-277-0702-8 58740
978-89-277-0701-1 58740 (set)

www.darakwon.co.kr

Components Main Book / Workbook
16 15 14 13 12 11 10   25 26 27 28 29

Developing Listening Skills

1

DARAKWON

Table of Contents

Introduction

Developing Listening Skills Book 1 is the first book in a four-book series. This book is intended for elementary learners of the English language. By using this book, learners will be able to improve their listening skills as well as their knowledge of English.

Developing Listening Skills Book 1 contains twenty units. The twenty units are divided into five topics, each of which contains four units. The five topics in *Developing Listening Skills Book 1* are Astronomy, Norse Mythology, Famous Discoveries, Great Books, and Unique Animals. These are all topics that young learners find interesting and enjoy learning about. So learners will have fun listening to the material in this book while improving their English at the same time.

Every unit contains one main talk, a shorter talk, and questions about these talks. Each unit also contains a listening skill and exercises on it. The listening skills will help learners improve various aspects of their listening abilities.

Developing Listening Skills Book 1 has several objectives. First, it will help learners improve their English abilities, particularly their listening skills. Next, it will teach them valuable knowledge about a wide range of academic topics. The talks themselves will also entertain learners as they listen to them. Finally, *Developing Listening Skills Book 1* will help learners prepare for various standardized tests that they may take in the future. For instance, many questions about the talks are similar to those that appear on the iBT TOEFL® Junior and iBT TOEFL® exams. So, by using this book, learners should be able to get higher scores on the tests they take in the future.

About This Book

There are a total of twenty units. Each unit contains one main talk about a specific topic. There are vocabulary and listening comprehension questions about the main talk. There is also a shorter talk with listening comprehension questions. There are a total of ten listening skills that are taught in the various chapters. Finally, there is a comprehensive vocabulary section as well as a workbook that will help learners increase their understanding of the talks and improve their English abilities.

Pre-Listening Questions

There are three questions that focus on the picture or pictures at the top of the page. These questions will help prepare learners for the topic of the unit.

Vocabulary

This section contains three vocabulary words from the main talk. Learners should match the words with the pictures.

Talk

This is the main talk of the unit. Each talk is around 220-250 words long and focuses on the topic of the unit.

Organizer

This is a graphic organizer of the talk. There are six blanks for learners to fill in by using words in the talk.

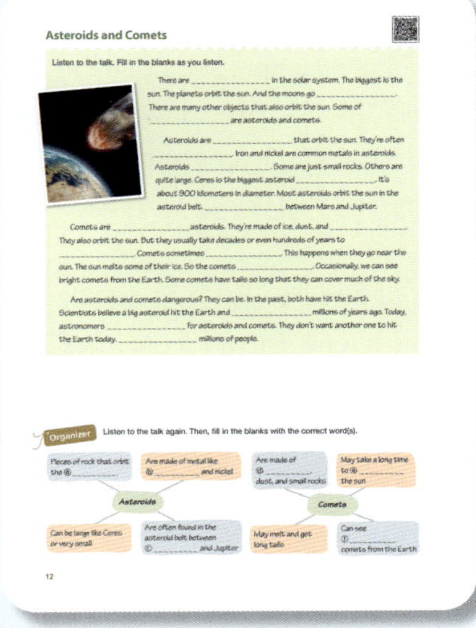

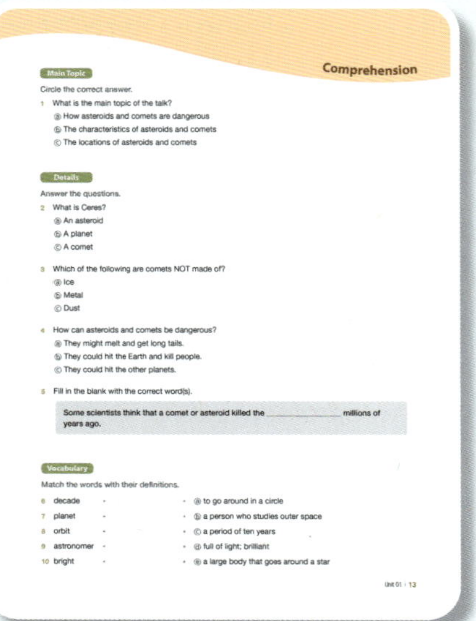

Comprehension

This page contains several questions about the main talk. There is a question about the main topic or main idea of the talk. There are also four questions that ask about the details in the talk. Finally, there are five vocabulary questions for learners to test their knowledge of the words in the talk.

Listening Skills Practice

This section provides further practice for learners. First, there is a listening skills section in each unit. Various listening skills, such as detail, chronological order, note-taking, dictation, and outlining, are covered in each unit. There is a description of the listening skill as well as questions for learners to test their understanding of the listening skill.

In addition, there is a short talk that is around 140-160 words long. Each talk provides information about a topic related to the main talk. There are comprehension questions and listening skill questions for each short talk as well.

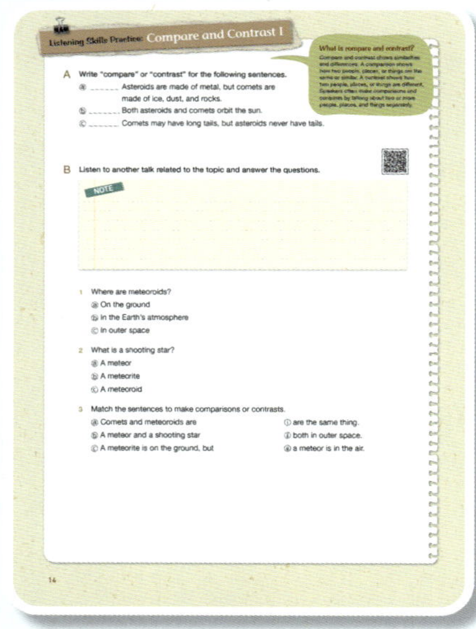

Chapter 1
Astronomy

Asteroids and Comets

Answer the following questions.

1   What is this picture of?

2   What are asteroids and comets?

3   Can asteroids and comets be dangerous?

Look at the pictures. Write the correct word(s) from the box for each picture.

asteroid	dinosaur	tail

1

2

3

Asteroids and Comets

Listen to the talk. Fill in the blanks as you listen.

There are _________________ in the solar system. The biggest is the sun. The planets orbit the sun. And the moons go _________________. There are many other objects that also orbit the sun. Some of _________________ are asteroids and comets.

Asteroids are _________________ that orbit the sun. They're often _________________. Iron and nickel are common metals in asteroids. Asteroids _________________. Some are just small rocks. Others are quite large. Ceres is the biggest asteroid _________________. It's about 900 kilometers in diameter. Most asteroids orbit the sun in the asteroid belt. _________________ between Mars and Jupiter.

Comets are _________________ asteroids. They're made of ice, dust, and _________________. They also orbit the sun. But they usually take decades or even hundreds of years to _________________. Comets sometimes _________________. This happens when they go near the sun. The sun melts some of their ice. So the comets _________________. Occasionally, we can see bright comets from the Earth. Some comets have tails so long that they can cover much of the sky.

Are asteroids and comets dangerous? They can be. In the past, both have hit the Earth. Scientists believe a big asteroid hit the Earth and _________________ millions of years ago. Today, astronomers _________________ for asteroids and comets. They don't want another one to hit the Earth today. _________________ millions of people.

Organizer — **Listen to the talk again. Then, fill in the blanks with the correct word(s).**

Pieces of rock that orbit the ⓐ _________

Are made of metal like ⓑ _________ and nickel

Are made of ⓓ _________, dust, and small rocks

May take a long time to ⓔ _________ the sun

Asteroids

Comets

Can be large like Ceres or very small

Are often found in the asteroid belt between ⓒ _________ and Jupiter

May melt and get long tails

Can see ⓕ _________ comets from the Earth

Main Topic

Circle the correct answer.

1   What is the main topic of the talk?

ⓐ How asteroids and comets are dangerous

ⓑ The characteristics of asteroids and comets

ⓒ The locations of asteroids and comets

Details

Answer the questions.

2   What is Ceres?

ⓐ An asteroid

ⓑ A planet

ⓒ A comet

3   Which of the following are comets NOT made of?

ⓐ Ice

ⓑ Metal

ⓒ Dust

4   How can asteroids and comets be dangerous?

ⓐ They might melt and get long tails.

ⓑ They could hit the Earth and kill people.

ⓒ They could hit the other planets.

5   Fill in the blank with the correct word(s).

Some scientists think that a comet or asteroid killed the ___________________ millions of years ago.

Vocabulary

Match the words with their definitions.

6   decade   •   •   ⓐ to go around in a circle

7   planet   •   •   ⓑ a person who studies outer space

8   orbit   •   •   ⓒ a period of ten years

9   astronomer   •   •   ⓓ full of light; brilliant

10   bright   •   •   ⓔ a large body that goes around a star

What is compare and contrast?
Compare and contrast shows similarities and differences. A comparison shows how two people, places, or things are the same or similar. A contrast shows how two people, places, or things are different. Speakers often make comparisons and contrasts by talking about two or more people, places, and things separately.

A Write "compare" or "contrast" for the following sentences.

ⓐ __________ Asteroids are made of metal, but comets are made of ice, dust, and rocks.

ⓑ __________ Both asteroids and comets orbit the sun.

ⓒ __________ Comets may have long tails, but asteroids never have tails.

B Listen to another talk related to the topic and answer the questions.

NOTE

1 Where are meteoroids?

ⓐ On the ground

ⓑ In the Earth's atmosphere

ⓒ In outer space

2 What is a shooting star?

ⓐ A meteor

ⓑ A meteorite

ⓒ A meteoroid

3 Match the sentences to make comparisons or contrasts.

ⓐ Comets and meteoroids are

ⓑ A meteor and a shooting star

ⓒ A meteorite is on the ground, but

ⓘ are the same thing.

ⓘⓘ both in outer space.

ⓘⓘⓘ a meteor is in the air.

02 Eclipses

Answer the following questions.

1. What are the objects in the picture?
2. How does an eclipse happen?
3. Have you ever seen an eclipse? What was it like?

Look at the pictures. Write the correct word(s) from the box for each picture.

blocked	solar system	revolve

1   2   3

________________   ________________   ________________

Eclipses

Listen to the talk. Fill in the blanks as you listen.

The objects in the solar system are ____________________.
For example, Earth moves around the sun. The other planets move around the sun, too. The moons move around various planets. For example, Earth's ____________________ around Earth. Sometimes ____________________ in space ____________________ with the sun. When this happens, there's an eclipse.

There are ____________________ eclipses. There are solar eclipses and lunar eclipses. A solar eclipse happens when the moon moves between ____________________. However, a lunar eclipse happens when ____________________ the moon and the sun. These two kinds of eclipses have ____________________.

For instance, solar eclipses are very rare. But lunar eclipses are ____________________. In addition, solar eclipses last for a short amount of time. They usually only last for ____________________. They can also only be seen in certain places on the planet. On the other hand, lunar eclipses can last for ____________________ of time. They may last for an hour and a half. Solar eclipses are more impressive than lunar eclipses though. During a lunar eclipse, the moon ____________________. It may look like it is red. During a solar eclipse, the sun's ____________________. So it becomes dark during the day. Solar eclipses can be dangerous. People shouldn't look directly at them. But it's okay to look straight at a lunar eclipse.

Organizer   **Listen to the talk again. Then, fill in the blanks with the correct word(s).**

Solar Eclipse

- Happens when the ⓐ ____________ moves between the sun and Earth
- Lasts for a few minutes
- Becomes ⓑ ____________ during the day
- Can be ⓒ ____________ if people look straight at it

Lunar Eclipse

- Happens when Earth moves ⓓ ____________ the moon and the sun
- Is more ⓔ ____________ than a solar eclipse
- May last up to an hour and a half
- May cause the moon to appear ⓕ ____________ in color

Main Topic

Circle the correct answer.

1   What is the main idea of the talk?

    ⓐ Some eclipses are dangerous to look at.

    ⓑ There are both solar and lunar eclipses.

    ⓒ Lunar eclipses are more common than solar eclipses.

Details

Answer the questions.

2   When does an eclipse happen?

    ⓐ When two objects form a line with the sun

    ⓑ When two objects form a line with Earth

    ⓒ When two objects form a line with the moon

3   How long does a solar eclipse last?

    ⓐ A few minutes

    ⓑ A few hours

    ⓒ A few days

4   Which is NOT true about lunar eclipses?

    ⓐ They may make the moon look red.

    ⓑ They can be dangerous to look at.

    ⓒ They happen more often than solar eclipses.

5   Fill in the blank with the correct word(s).

> **People should not look straight at ________________ eclipses because that can be dangerous.**

Vocabulary

Match the words and phrases with their definitions.

6   look directly at •   • ⓐ continual; happening all the time

7   last •   • ⓑ related to the sun

8   solar •   • ⓒ to take a certain amount of time

9   lunar •   • ⓓ related to the moon

10   constant •   • ⓔ to look straight at

What is compare and contrast?
Compare and contrast shows similarities and differences. A comparison shows how two people, places, or things are the same or similar. A contrast shows how two people, places, or things are different. *And*, *both*, and *also* are common words in comparisons. *But*, *however*, and *yet* are common words in contrasts.

A Fill in the blanks with the correct word from the box.

both	and	but

ⓐ Solar eclipses are rare, _________________ lunar eclipses are more common.

ⓑ _________________ solar and lunar eclipses involve the sun, moon, and Earth.

ⓒ Lunar eclipses last around an hour and a half, _________________ solar eclipses are even shorter.

B Listen to a news broadcast related to the topic and answer the questions.

Memo

1 How long will the eclipse last?

ⓐ Five minutes

ⓑ Ten minutes

ⓒ Twenty-two minutes

2 What kind of eclipse is going to happen?

ⓐ A near eclipse

ⓑ A partial eclipse

ⓒ A total eclipse

3 Circle the correct word in each sentence.

ⓐ A partial eclipse blocks some light; (however / so), a total eclipse blocks most of the sun's light.

ⓑ (Neither / Both) total and partial eclipses are kinds of solar eclipses.

ⓒ Total eclipses are dangerous to look at, (but / and) partial eclipses are dangerous, too.

Galileo Galilei

Answer the following questions.

1 Who was Galileo Galilei?

2 What can you see in the second picture?

3 What do you think the moons in the solar system orbit?

Look at the pictures. Write the correct word(s) from the box for each picture.

mathematician	tutor	telescope

1 

2

3

_______________________   _______________________   _______________________

Galileo Galilei

Listen to the talk. Fill in the blanks as you listen.

Galileo Galilei was born in Pisa, Italy, in 1564. He lived during the Renaissance. This was a time of _____________________ in Europe. Education was very important then. So Galileo's father _____________________ for him. Galileo studied hard and learned a lot. He had _____________________ his life. He was an astronomer, mathematician, inventor, and physicist. But most people today _____________________ his work in astronomy.

Galileo was really interested _____________________. He wanted to _____________________ them. He heard about _____________________: eyeglasses. Galileo decided to make his own. The result was _____________________. Galileo used his new invention to look at the night sky. Thanks to it, he could see objects _____________________.

Galileo looked at the moon. He saw many of its craters. Then, he looked at Jupiter. He saw four tiny objects around it. These were Jupiter's _____________________. Today, they are called the Galilean moons. More notably, Galileo realized that they were _____________________. In the past, people believed that everything in the sky—the sun, stars, moon, and planets—orbited Earth. This was called the geocentric model of the universe. Galileo realized that _____________________. He believed in a new theory. It was called the heliocentric model of the universe. It stated that the objects in the solar system _____________________, not Earth. Many people _____________________ Galileo. But this model of the universe was correct.

Organizer   **Listen to the talk again. Then, fill in the blanks with the correct word(s).**

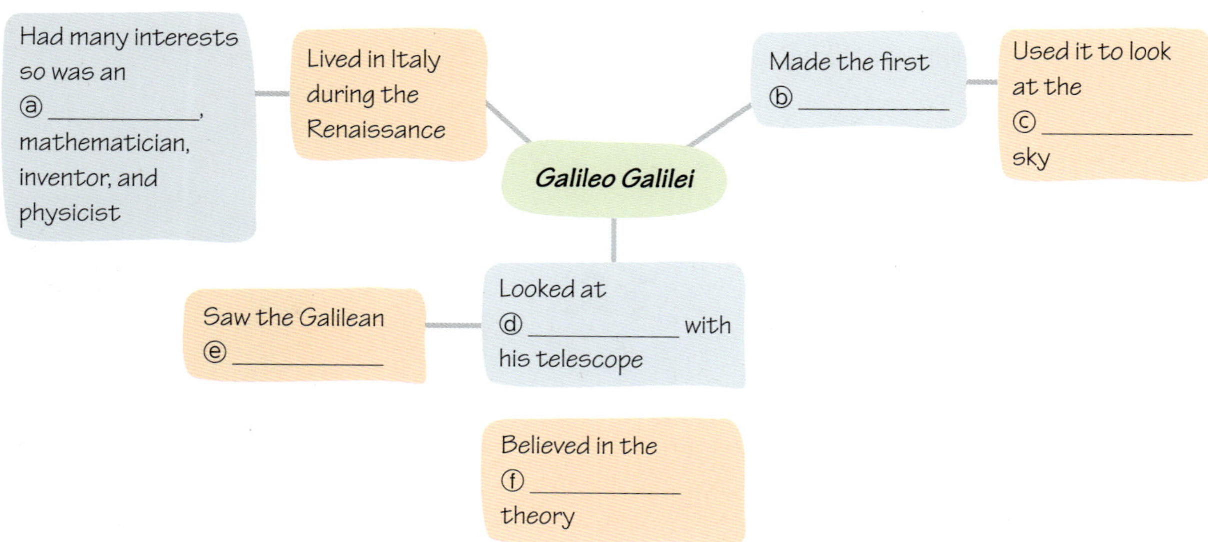

Circle the correct answer.

1   What is the main idea of the talk?

ⓐ The moons of the planet Jupiter orbit it.

ⓑ The heliocentric model is the correct model of the universe.

ⓒ Galileo was an important astronomer in the past.

Details

Answer the questions.

2   Which of the following did Galileo NOT do?

ⓐ He invented new things.

ⓑ He discovered Jupiter.

ⓒ He studied math.

3   What did Galileo make?

ⓐ The telescope

ⓑ Eyeglasses

ⓒ The microscope

4   What is the geocentric model of the universe?

ⓐ The idea that everything orbits the sun

ⓑ The idea that everything orbits the planets

ⓒ The idea that everything orbits Earth

5   Fill in the blank with the correct word(s).

Galileo looked at the planet ___________________ and discovered four of its moons.

Vocabulary

Match the words and phrases with their definitions.

6   geocentric   ⓐ the sky with the stars, moon, and planets in it

7   heliocentric   ⓑ learning

8   crater   ⓒ centered on the Earth

9   night sky   ⓓ a large hole in a surface

10 education   ⓔ centered on the sun

> **What is outlining?**
> Outlining is a way to summarize the main points of a talk. An outline does not need sentences. Instead, it uses short phrases and words. Always write down the main ideas or actions in the talk. Then, write down the main details in the talk. There may be one, two, or three main details for each main idea or action. Do not write down minor details. They are not important.

A Listen to the talk again. Then, complete the outline by using the words in the box.

orbited	inventor	geocentric	discovered	Renaissance

Galileo Galilei

I. Lived during the ⓐ _____________
   i. Was a time of learning in Europe
   ii. Galileo studied hard
   iii. Was an astronomer, mathematician, ⓑ _____________, and physicist

II. Invented the first telescope
   i. Looked at the craters of the moon
   ii. ⓒ _____________ Jupiter's four biggest moons

III. Believed in the heliocentric model of the universe
   i. Saw that moons ⓓ _____________ Jupiter
   ii. Replaced the ⓔ _____________ model of the universe

B Listen to another talk related to the topic and answer the questions.

NOTE

1 Complete the outline by filling in the blanks.

Telescopes

I. Are many kinds of telescopes
II. ⓐ _____________ telescopes
   i. First made by Galileo
   ii. Use ⓑ _____________
   iii. Excellent for looking at ⓒ _____________ objects and bright stars
   iv. Cost a lot of money

III. Reflecting telescopes
   i. First made by Sir Isaac Newton
   ii. Collect light with ⓓ _____________
   iii. Good for looking at ⓔ _____________ objects

IV. Do not cost a lot of ⓕ _____________

2 How are reflecting telescopes different from refracting telescopes?

ⓐ Reflecting telescopes are more expensive.

ⓑ Reflecting telescopes are good for looking at nearby objects.

ⓒ Reflecting telescopes are larger in size.

Percival Lowell

Answer the following questions.

1   What can you see in both pictures?

2   What are the names of the planets in the solar system?

3   Do you think there is life on other planets?

Look at the pictures. Write the correct word(s) from the box for each picture.

Mars	orbit	canal

1   

2

3

_______________   _______________   _______________

Percival Lowell

Listen to the talk. Fill in the blanks as you listen.

In the 1800s, there were ___________________. They made many people ___________________ science. One of those people was Percival Lowell. He was born ___________________ and died in 1916. Lowell focused much of his life on astronomy. Today, people remember him for two things: ___________________.

In the 1800s, people were fascinated with Mars. They often ___________________ there was life on that planet. There were lots of books and stories about Mars in popular culture. *The War of the Worlds* by H.G. Wells was the most famous one. Lowell spent more than fifteen years studying Mars. He ___________________ it with telescopes. He ___________________ on the planet. Lowell thought ___________________. So he believed there was ___________________. He even wrote a couple of books about Mars. They were very popular with the reading public. Unfortunately, there was no life on Mars. So Lowell ___________________ that.

He wasn't, however, wrong about Pluto. For centuries, people knew about ___________________. They knew about Mercury, Venus, Mars, Jupiter, and Saturn. Then, in 1781, Uranus was discovered. In 1846, Neptune was located. Lowell studied the orbits of both planets. He thought that the gravity of ___________________ was affecting them. He called it Planet X. In 1906, Lowell ___________________ Planet X. He continued his search until he died. He never found it. But others kept searching. In 1930, Clyde Tombaugh ___________________. It was ___________________ Pluto.

Organizer Listen to the talk again. Then, fill in the blanks with the correct word(s).

Percival Lowell

Was interested in ⓐ ___________ — Studied it for ⓑ ___________ years — Thought he saw ⓒ ___________ — Believed there was life on Mars

Wanted to find Planet X — Studied the orbits of ⓓ ___________ and Neptune — Thought that Planet X was ⓔ ___________ them — Searched for Planet X from 1906 until he died — Was found in 1930 and called ⓕ ___________

Main Topic

Circle the correct answer.

1   What is the main topic of the talk?

    ⓐ The discovery of Pluto by Clyde Tombaugh

    ⓑ The work in astronomy that Percival Lowell did

    ⓒ The possibility that there is life on Mars

Details

Answer the questions.

2   What did Percival Lowell think that the lines on Mars were?

    ⓐ Roads

    ⓑ Canals

    ⓒ Rivers

3   Why did Percival Lowell believe there was another planet in the solar system?

    ⓐ He found some images of strange objects when using his telescopes.

    ⓑ He wanted to become famous by finding a new planet.

    ⓒ He thought an unknown planet was affecting Uranus and Neptune.

4   Which person did NOT search for Planet X?

    ⓐ Carl Sagan

    ⓑ Clyde Tombaugh

    ⓒ Percival Lowell

5   Fill in the blank with the correct word(s).

> After Planet X was found, it was later named ___________________.

Vocabulary

Match the words and phrases with their definitions.

6   numerous •   • ⓐ large in number; very many

7   continue •   • ⓑ to keep doing something

8   reading public •   • ⓒ amazed

9   fascinated •   • ⓓ a development; a move forward

10   advance •   • ⓔ the people who read

What is outlining?
Outlining is a way to summarize the main points of a talk. An outline does not need sentences. Instead, it uses short phrases and words. Focus on the main ideas or actions in the talk. Write them down. Then, write down the details that are related to the main ideas or actions. Ignore the minor points and details. They are not important for an outline.

A Listen to the talk again. Then, complete the outline by using the words in the box.

Clyde Tombaugh	Mars	solar system	canals	Planet X

Percival Lowell

I. Focused much of his life on astronomy
II. Mars
  i. Studied ⓐ ______________ for fifteen years
  ii. Looked at it with telescopes
  iii. Thought lines on planet were ⓑ ______________
  iv. Believed there was life on Mars

III. Planet X
  i. Believed there was another planet in the ⓒ ______________
  ii. Thought the planet was affecting Uranus and Neptune
  iii. Looked for ⓓ ______________ from 1906 until he died
IV. Was found by ⓔ ______________ in 1930 and named Pluto

B Listen to a talk by an announcer related to the topic and answer the questions.

Memo

1 Complete the outline by filling in the blanks.

The Debate on Mars

I. Answer the question "Was there ever ⓐ ______________ on Mars?"
II. Professor Mark Chapman
  i. Believes there was life on Mars in the ⓑ ______________
  ii. Thinks there is no life on Mars now

  iii. Says the life on Mars ⓒ ______________ a long time ago
III. Professor Susan Perkins
  i. Says there has ⓓ ______________ been life on Mars
  ii. Thinks the only life in the ⓔ ______________ is on Earth

2 Where is the debate being held?
  ⓐ At a school
  ⓑ In a library
  ⓒ In a coffee shop

Chapter 2
Norse Mythology

05 Norse Gods and Goddesses

Pre-Listening Questions

Answer the following questions.

1   What are the names of the gods and goddesses in the pictures?

2   What do you know about Norse mythology?

3   Do you know any stories from mythology in your country? What are they?

Vocabulary

Look at the pictures. Write the correct word(s) from the box for each picture.

warrior	battle	Scandinavia

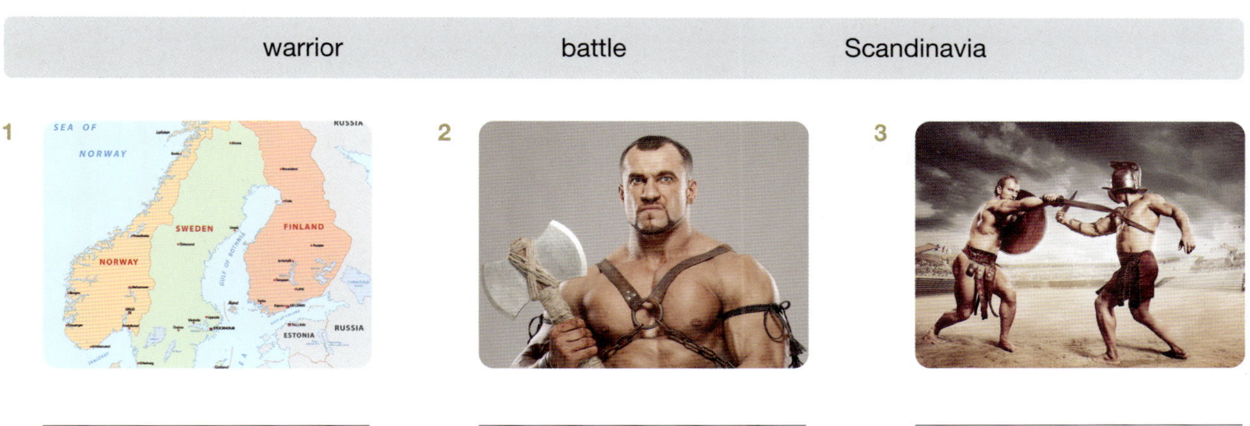

1   __________________

2   __________________

3   __________________

Norse Gods and Goddesses

Listen to the talk. Fill in the blanks as you listen.

Many people ____________________ the Greek gods and goddesses. A lot of people know about the Roman gods and goddesses, too. But ____________________ the Norse gods and goddesses. Norse mythology ____________________ Scandinavia. Denmark, Norway, Sweden, and Finland are all in Scandinavia.

There were many gods and goddesses in Norse mythology. Odin was one of them. Odin was the father of all ____________________. He was a very wise god. He only had ____________________. He often had two ravens with him. Their names were Hugin and Munin. Another well-known god was Thor. Thor was the strongest and ____________________ of the Norse gods. He protected Midgard. It was the land where humans lived. He carried ____________________ and was known as the Thunderer. Loki was another god. He was the trickster god. In many Norse myths, Loki caused a lot of the problems the gods ____________________. Some other Norse gods were Tyr, Freyr, and Heimdall.

Goddesses were also important in Norse mythology. Freya was the goddess of love and beauty. But she was also ____________________. Frigga was Odin's wife and was the ____________________. Skadi was the goddess of winter. Hel was the goddess of ____________________.

There were many other gods and goddesses in Norse mythology. They often ____________________ and other monsters. Their stories are often ____________________.

Organizer   **Listen to the talk again. Then, fill in the blanks with the correct word(s).**

Norse Gods

Odin: the one-eyed wise god who was the ⓐ ____________ of all gods and men

ⓑ ____________ : the strong, powerful god who protected Midgard

Loki: the ⓒ ____________ god who caused many problems

Norse Goddesses

Freya: the goddess of ⓓ ____________ and beauty and a warrior goddess

Frigga: Odin's ⓔ ____________ and the protector of children

Skadi: the goddess of ⓕ ____________

Hel: the goddess of the underworld

Main Topic

Circle the correct answer.

1 What is the main topic of the talk?

    ⓐ The strongest gods in Norse mythology

    ⓑ The gods and goddesses in Norse mythology

    ⓒ The powers of the goddesses in Norse mythology

Details

Answer the questions.

2 Which is NOT true about Odin?

    ⓐ He had two ravens named Hugin and Munin.

    ⓑ He was the father of all gods and men.

    ⓒ He was the strongest and most powerful god.

3 Who was the trickster god?

    ⓐ Loki

    ⓑ Thor

    ⓒ Heimdall

4 What was Freya the goddess of?

    ⓐ The underworld

    ⓑ Love and beauty

    ⓒ Winter

5 Fill in the blank with the correct word(s).

> People in ___________________ told stories about the Norse gods and goddesses.

Vocabulary

Match the words and phrases with their definitions.

6 trickster   •   • ⓐ to be called

7 protect   •   • ⓑ a person who plays jokes or tricks on others

8 mythology   •   • ⓒ the land beneath the surface of the Earth

9 underworld   •   • ⓓ to guard; to take care of; to keep safe

10 be known as   •   • ⓔ legends; stories from the past that may or may not be true

What is note-taking?

Note-taking is a way to organize and write down important information in a talk. Do not write sentences when you take notes. Instead, listen carefully to the speaker. Be sure to focus on the key words and phrases the person says. Write down only the important information. Ignore all of the minor points or unimportant information.

A Circle the important words and phrases in each sentence.

ⓐ Norse mythology comes from Scandinavia. Denmark, Norway, Sweden, and Finland are all in Scandinavia.

ⓑ Odin was the father of all gods and men. He was a very wise god.

ⓒ Freya was the goddess of love and beauty. But she was also a warrior goddess.

B Listen to another talk related to the topic and answer the questions.

1 What does "Midgard" mean?
ⓐ Higher Earth
ⓑ Middle Earth
ⓒ Lower Earth

2 What connected Asgard with Midgard?
ⓐ A wooden bridge
ⓑ A stone bridge
ⓒ A rainbow bridge

3 Listen to the talk again. Take notes on the following topics.
ⓐ Asgard: _______________________________________
ⓑ Jotunheim: ____________________________________
ⓒ Yggdrasil: _____________________________________

Creatures in Norse Mythology

Pre-Listening Questions

Answer the following questions.

1   What creatures are in the pictures?

2   What are some other creatures in Norse mythology?

3   Do you know any creatures from your country's mythology?

Vocabulary

Look at the pictures. Write the correct word(s) from the box for each picture.

claws	fangs	dragon

1 
2 
3

Creatures in Norse Mythology

Listen to the talk. Fill in the blanks as you listen.

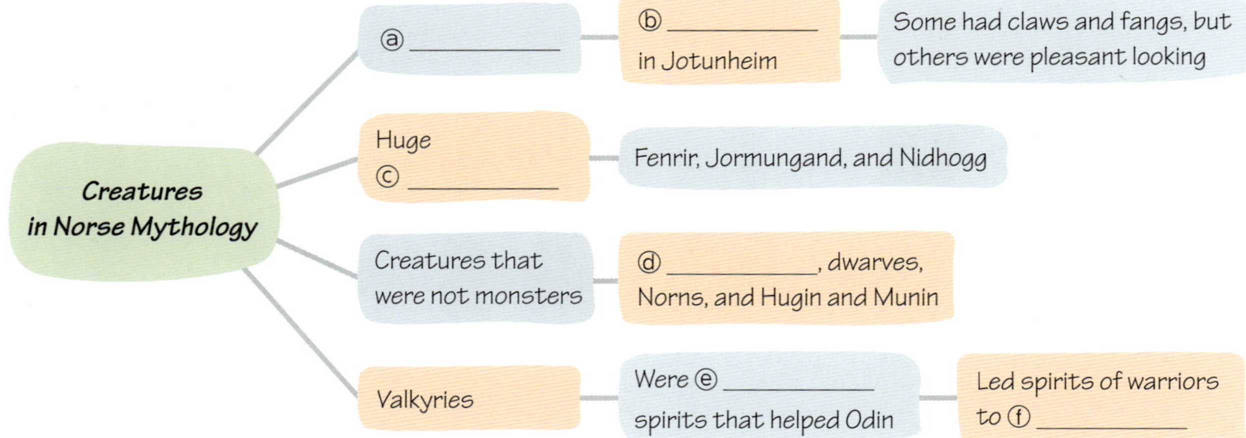

There are lots of gods and goddesses in Norse mythology. There are many
__________________, too. __________________, but others aren't.

The Norse gods and goddesses often battled the giants. The giants
__________________ the land of Jotunheim. But they frequently left
Jotunheim to cause problems. The giants had a variety of appearances.
Most of them were __________________. Some had claws, and
__________________. But a few of them were actually pleasant to look at.

Many of the monsters in Norse mythology were huge. There was
__________________ named Fenrir. There was also an enormous sea
serpent called Jormungand. And Nidhogg was __________________ snake or a dragon. It was
always __________________ part of the world tree Yggdrasil.

Fortunately, not all of the creatures in Norse mythology were monsters. There were elves that lived
__________________ and dwarves that lived beneath it. The Norns were __________________ who
were very __________________. They were able to influence the destinies of people. Odin had two
ravens called Hugin and Munin. They flew around the world every day while __________________. Then,
they __________________ they saw and heard to Odin.

Finally, there were the Valkyries. These were female spirits that assisted Odin. They
__________________ on the battlefield. When the men died, the Valkyries led the spirits of the
__________________ men to Valhalla. This was __________________ of the dead for the greatest
warriors.

Organizer Listen to the talk again. Then, fill in the blanks with the correct word(s).

Creatures in Norse Mythology

- ⓐ __________ → ⓑ __________ in Jotunheim → Some had claws and fangs, but others were pleasant looking
- Huge ⓒ __________ → Fenrir, Jormungand, and Nidhogg
- Creatures that were not monsters → ⓓ __________, dwarves, Norns, and Hugin and Munin
- Valkyries → Were ⓔ __________ spirits that helped Odin → Led spirits of warriors to ⓕ __________

Main Topic

Circle the correct answer.

1   What is the main idea of the talk?

    ⓐ There were both good and bad creatures in Norse mythology.

    ⓑ The giants often fought battles against the Valkyries.

    ⓒ Some of the creatures in Norse mythology could use magic.

Details

Answer the questions.

2   What was Jormungand?

    ⓐ A giant wolf

    ⓑ A sea serpent

    ⓒ A dragon

3   What did Hugin and Munin do?

    ⓐ They reported information to Odin.

    ⓑ They fought against the giants.

    ⓒ They worked with the elves and dwarves.

4   What is NOT true about the Valkyries?

    ⓐ They took warriors to Valhalla.

    ⓑ They were female spirits.

    ⓒ They worked closely with Thor.

5   Fill in the blank with the correct word(s).

> Some giants had fangs and claws, but others were _________________ to look at.

Vocabulary

Match the words and phrases with their definitions.

6   sea serpent   •   • ⓐ a place where a battle is fought

7   dwarf   •   • ⓑ very large; huge; enormous

8   battlefield   •   • ⓒ fate; what will happen to someone in the future

9   destiny   •   • ⓓ a very large snake that lives in the water

10 gigantic   •   • ⓔ a small creature that looks like a human and lives underground

What is note-taking?
Note-taking is a way to organize and write down important information in a talk. Do not write sentences when you take notes. Instead, listen carefully to the speaker. Be sure to focus on the key words and phrases the person says. Do not write words like *a*, *an*, and *the*. Do not write verbs like *am*, *is*, and *are* either.

A Circle the important words and phrases in each sentence.

ⓐ The giants had a variety of appearances. Most of them were very large. Some had claws, and others had fangs.

ⓑ There was a gigantic wolf named Fenrir. There was also an enormous sea serpent called Jormungand.

ⓒ Finally, there were the Valkyries. These were female spirits that assisted Odin.

B Listen to a school report related to the topic and answer the questions.

1 What did Fenrir look like?

ⓐ A bear

ⓑ A wolf

ⓒ An eagle

2 Why were the gods afraid of Fenrir?

ⓐ He killed one of the gods.

ⓑ He was friends with the giants.

ⓒ He was very dangerous.

3 Listen to the talk again. Take notes on the following topics.
ⓐ Loki: ____
ⓑ dwarves: ____
ⓒ Tyr: ____

Unit 07 — Thor's Wedding

Answer the following questions.

1   Who is in the picture?
2   What do you know about Thor?
3   What do you think happens at Thor's wedding?

Look at the pictures. Write the correct word(s) from the box for each picture.

frost giant	veil	hammer

1

2

3

Thor's Wedding

Listen to the talk. Fill in the blanks as you listen.

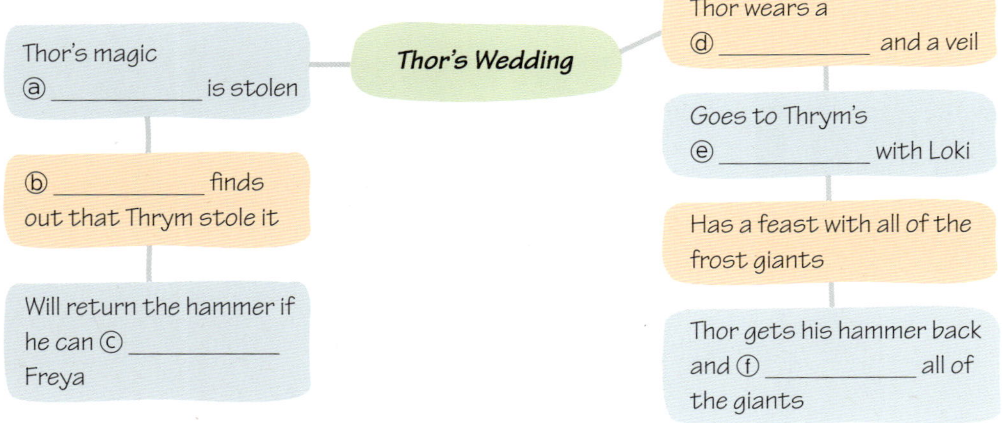

One morning, the god Thor woke up. He suddenly realized that his ___________________. Thor's hammer was a ___________________ that made him very powerful. He often used it to defeat his enemies in battle. Thor was upset, so he asked Loki ___________________.

Loki began ___________________ Thor's hammer. He soon learned that Thrym had stolen it. Thrym was the king of the frost giants. Thrym told Loki he would give back Thor's hammer. But, ___________________, Freya, the goddess of love and beauty, ___________________ him.

Freya ___________________ Thrym, but Loki thought of a clever plan. Loki told Thor to ___________________ a bridal gown. Then, he put a veil over Thor's face. ___________________, Thor and Loki went to Thrym's palace. Thrym thought Thor was Freya. He was very happy, so he prepared a great feast.

At the feast, the giants were surprised. Thor, who was disguised as Freya, ate a ___________________ food. Loki explained that Freya had not eaten for ___________________, so she was ___________________. Then, Thrym tried to kiss his bride. He ___________________ the veil but saw Thor's red eyes. Loki explained that Freya had ___________________ eight nights, so she had red eyes.

Finally, Thrym ___________________ to give Thor's hammer to Freya. They put the hammer ___________________. Thor immediately ___________________ and hit Thrym with it. Then, he killed all of the other giants in the palace, too.

Organizer Listen to the talk again. Then, fill in the blanks with the correct word(s).

Thor's magic ⓐ ___________ is stolen

Thor's Wedding

ⓑ ___________ finds out that Thrym stole it

Will return the hammer if he can ⓒ ___________ Freya

Thor wears a ⓓ ___________ and a veil

Goes to Thrym's ⓔ ___________ with Loki

Has a feast with all of the frost giants

Thor gets his hammer back and ⓕ ___________ all of the giants

Main Topic

Circle the correct answer.

1 What is the main topic of the talk?

ⓐ Why Thor got married to a frost giant

ⓑ The marriage of Thor and Freya

ⓒ How Thor got his hammer back from the frost giants

Details

Answer the questions.

2 What did Thrym steal from Thor?

ⓐ His veil

ⓑ His hammer

ⓒ His wife

3 Who thought of the idea to get Thor's hammer back?

ⓐ Loki

ⓑ Freya

ⓒ Thor

4 What did NOT happen at the feast at Thrym's palace?

ⓐ Thor killed all of the frost giants with his hammer.

ⓑ Thrym tried to kiss his bride but saw red eyes.

ⓒ The frost giants were impressed by Freya's beauty.

5 Fill in the blank with the correct word(s).

> **Thor had a magic hammer that he used when he fought his ___________________.**

Vocabulary

Match the words and phrases with their definitions.

6 bridal gown　　•　　　　•　ⓐ to command; to tell someone to do something

7 defeat　　•　　　　•　ⓑ a wedding dress

8 order　　•　　　　•　ⓒ to appear to be a different person

9 feast　　•　　　　•　ⓓ to win against; to beat

10 be disguised as　　•　　　　•　ⓔ a dinner with a great amount of food

What is problem and solution?
Problem and solution shows both a problem and how a person can solve it. First, listen carefully for the problem. Figure out what is wrong. Then, listen for what the person does to solve the problem. That is the solution. There are sometimes two or more problems and solutions in a talk.

A Listen to the talk again. Then, write P (problem) or S (solution).

ⓐ __________ Thor dressed up as Freya and went to Thrym's palace.

ⓑ __________ Thor grabbed the hammer and killed the giants with it.

ⓒ __________ Thrym stole Thor's magic hammer.

B Listen to another talk related to the topic and answer the questions.

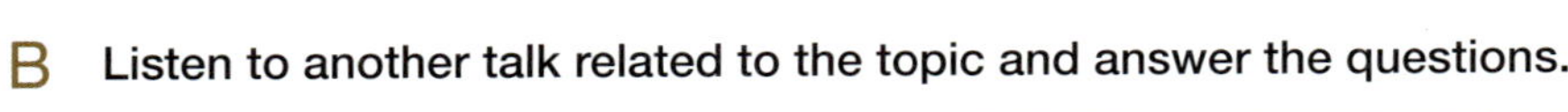

> NOTE

1 What did Odin love?

ⓐ Strength

ⓑ Power

ⓒ Wisdom

2 What did Odin give Mimir?

ⓐ Some water from the well

ⓑ One of his eyes

ⓒ His ravens Hugin and Munin

3 Match the sentences to find the problem and the solutions. Then, write P (problem) or S (solution) next to each sentence.

ⓐ __________ Odin took a drink   ⓘ become wiser.

ⓑ __________ Odin wanted to   ⓙ and dropped it in the well.

ⓒ __________ Odin cut out his eye   ⓚ of water from Mimir's Well.

Ragnarok

Answer the following questions.

1   Who is in the picture?

2   What is everyone doing?

3   Does your country have any myths about the end of the world? What are they?

Look at the pictures. Write the correct word(s) from the box for each picture.

poison	burn	captivity

1   

2

3

_______________   _______________   _______________

Ragnarok

Listen to the talk. Fill in the blanks as you listen.

Most cultures have stories ___________________ of the world. In Norse mythology, the name of this event is Ragnarok. It means "fate of the gods." It tells how the gods and their allies fight monsters at ___________________ at the end of the world. ___________________ life on the Earth dies during Ragnarok.

First, there will be a time called Fimbulwinter. There will be three years of winter ___________________. Next, the sun and stars will disappear, and the Earth will ___________________. Then, Fenrir the wolf will ___________________ captivity. He will ___________________ Loki, the giants, and many other monsters. They will all travel to Vigrid. They will battle the Norse gods at Vigrid.

The gods will see the armies approaching. They will ___________________ and go to fight their enemies. According to Norse mythology, the gods ___________________ who they will fight and who will die. For example, Fenrir will kill Odin ___________________. Thor will slay Jormungand the sea serpent ___________________. But Jormungand's ___________________ Thor. Heimdall and Loki will fight and kill each other.

At the end of the battle, the sky will burn. The Earth will ___________________ the sea. However, that isn't the end of the world. A new Earth will ___________________ the sea. Some gods will survive the battle, too. And two humans will survive. They will restart ___________________.

Organizer Listen to the talk again. Then, fill in the blanks with the correct word(s).

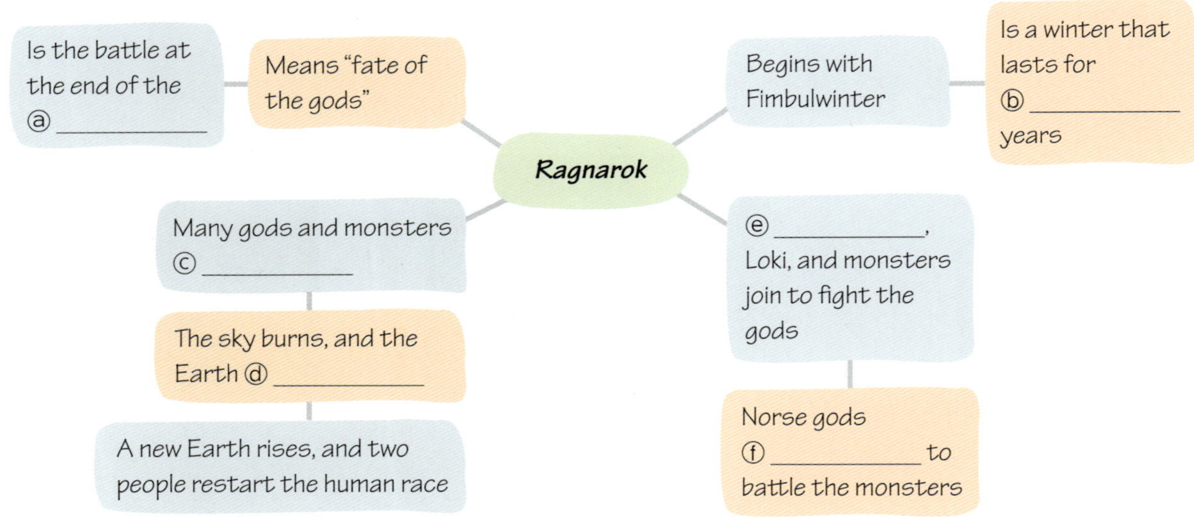

Main Topic

Circle the correct answer.

1   What is the main idea of the talk?
  ⓐ Many of the Norse gods are going to die.
  ⓑ There will be a great battle at Ragnarok.
  ⓒ Fimbulwinter will be a very cold period.

Details

Answer the questions.

2   What does Ragnarok mean?
  ⓐ Battle of the gods
  ⓑ Death of the gods
  ⓒ Fate of the gods

3   What is NOT going to happen during Ragnarok?
  ⓐ Odin is going to kill Fenrir.
  ⓑ Loki is going to die in a fight.
  ⓒ Thor is going to kill Jormungand.

4   What will happen after the battle ends?
  ⓐ All humans will die.
  ⓑ The gods will come back to life.
  ⓒ A new Earth will rise above the water.

5   Fill in the blank with the correct word(s).

> **Many monsters will join to fight against the Norse ______________ during Ragnarok.**

Vocabulary

Match the words with their definitions.

6   slay   •   • ⓐ to begin again

7   sink   •   • ⓑ to kill

8   battle   •   • ⓒ a fight

9   restart   •   • ⓓ to vanish; to go away

10 disappear   •   • ⓔ to go beneath the surface of the water

A Listen to the talk again. Then, write P (problem) or S (solution).

ⓐ __________ Many monsters join to form an army to fight the gods.

ⓑ __________ The Norse gods get ready for battle.

ⓒ __________ The gods fight various monsters and enemies and kill them.

B Listen to a student presentation related to the topic and answer the questions.

1 Who is Hymir?

ⓐ A god

ⓑ A giant

ⓒ A whale

2 What do Thor and Hymir do together?

ⓐ They go fishing.

ⓑ They go hunting.

ⓒ They go swimming.

3 Match the sentences to find the problem and the solutions. Then, write P (problem) or S (solution) next to each sentence.

ⓐ __________ Thor and Hymir agree   ⓘ to go fishing together.

ⓑ __________ Thor eats too much   ⓘⓘ a couple of whales.

ⓒ __________ Hymir catches   ⓘⓘⓘ food at Hymir's house.

Chapter 3
Famous Discoveries

King Tut's Tomb

Answer the following questions.

1   What can you see in the pictures?

2   Who was King Tut?

3   What do you know about ancient Egypt?

Look at the pictures. Write the correct word(s) from the box for each picture.

ivory	pharaoh	mummy

1

2

3

King Tut's Tomb

Listen to the talk. Fill in the blanks as you listen.

In 1341 B.C., Pharaoh Amenhotep IV had a son. He _____________________ Tutankhamen. Nine years later, Amenhotep had to _____________________ the throne. So, in 1332 B.C., Tutankhamen became the new pharaoh. King Tut was just _____________________. There were no exciting events during his reign. And he was only pharaoh _____________________. In 1323 B.C., when he was _____________________, King Tut died.

After he died, King Tut's body _____________________ a mummy. Then, the Egyptians took him to the Valley of the Kings. They buried many pharaohs and other nobles there. King Tut's mummy and many valuable treasures were sealed _____________________. Over time, the desert sands buried his tomb. And King Tut _____________________ people's memories.

More than 3,000 years later, Howard Carter _____________________ 1874. In 1892, at the age of seventeen, Carter made _____________________ to Egypt. On that trip, he _____________________ of Egyptian tombs. He also fell in love with Egypt. So Carter made studying it his goal in life.

In 1917, Carter began excavating areas in the Valley of the Kings. For several years, he _____________________. Then, in November 1922, he _____________________. It led to King Tut's tomb. On November 26, 1922, he _____________________. It was mostly in good condition. King Tut's mummy was there. There were jewelry, gold and _____________________, and other valuable objects. Carter's partner asked him, "Can you see anything?" Carter responded, "Yes, wonderful things."

Organizer   Listen to the talk again. Then, fill in the blanks with the correct word(s).

King Tut

- Was the son of Pharaoh Amenhotep IV
- Was born in 1341 B.C.
- Was turned into a ⓐ _____________ and buried in the Valley of the Kings
- Was ⓑ _____________ from 1332 B.C. to 1323 B.C.

Howard Carter

- Was ⓒ _____________ in 1874
- Fell in love with ⓓ _____________ and studied it
- Opened King Tut's ⓔ _____________ on November 26, 1922
- Began ⓕ _____________ in the Valley of the Kings in 1917

Main Topic

Circle the correct answer.

1   What is the main topic of the talk?
   ⓐ King Tut and the discovery of his tomb
   ⓑ King Tut and the story of his life
   ⓒ The lives of King Tut and Howard Carter

Details

Answer the questions.

2   How old was King Tut when he became the pharaoh?
   ⓐ Around four
   ⓑ Around nine
   ⓒ Around nineteen

3   Where did Howard Carter find King Tut's tomb?
   ⓐ Near Cairo
   ⓑ By the Great Pyramid of Giza
   ⓒ In the Valley of the Kings

4   What did Howard Carter NOT find in King Tut's tomb?
   ⓐ King Tut's wife's mummy
   ⓑ Jewelry
   ⓒ King Tut's mummy

5   Fill in the blank with the correct word(s).

> When Howard Carter opened King Tut's tomb, he said that he saw "______________ things."

Vocabulary

Match the words and phrases with their definitions.

6   bury   •   •   ⓐ the place where a dead body is put

7   tomb   •   •   ⓑ to dig up from the ground

8   excavate   •   •   ⓒ to put underground and to cover with dirt

9   reign   •   •   ⓓ to come to like very much

10 fall in love with   •   •   ⓔ the time when a king or queen rules

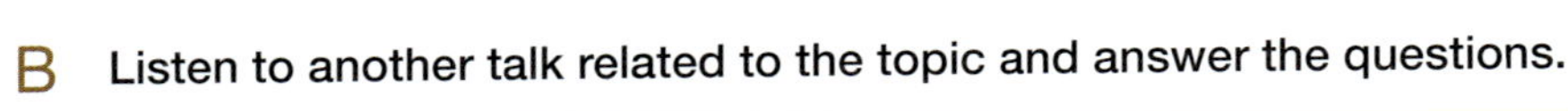

What is chronological order?
Chronological order is a way to put events in order. By using chronological order, the events are put in the order that they happened. So time is very important for chronological order. Many times, a talk includes days, years, dates, and times. Use this information to put the events in the talk in the correct chronological order.

A Listen to the talk again. Then, put the sentences in chronological order.

ⓐ _________ In 1922, Howard Carter discovered King Tut's tomb.

ⓑ _________ In 1332 B.C., King Tut became the new pharaoh.

ⓒ _________ Howard Carter was born in 1874.

B Listen to another talk related to the topic and answer the questions.

> NOTE

1 Why was Petra unique?

ⓐ It was built on a mountain.

ⓑ It was built in a valley.

ⓒ It was built beside a lake.

2 What did Johann Burckhardt do?

ⓐ He rediscovered the lost city of Petra.

ⓑ He founded the city of Petra.

ⓒ He lived in the city of Petra.

3 Write the correct years in the blanks. Then, put the sentences in chronological order.

ⓐ _________ In __________________, people settled in the land around Petra.

ⓑ _________ Johann Burckhardt found the lost city of Petra in __________________.

ⓒ _________ In the __________________, the city of Petra was built.

The Rosetta Stone

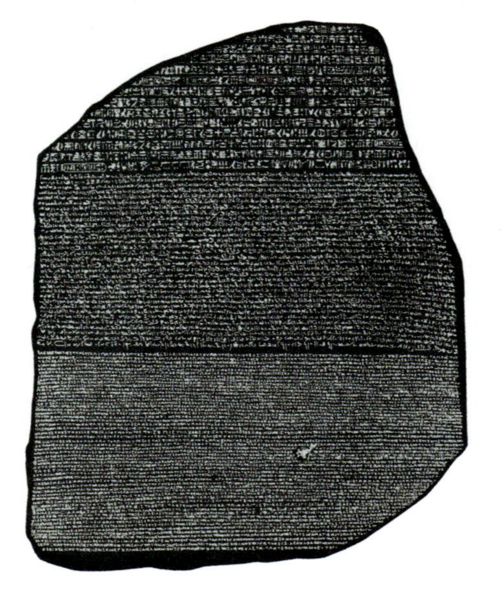

Answer the following questions.

1   What is the Rosetta Stone?

2   Why is the Rosetta Stone important?

3   What do you know about hieroglyphics?

Look at the pictures. Write the correct word(s) from the box for each picture.

ruins	text	hieroglyphics

1 

2

3

The Rosetta Stone

Listen to the talk. Fill in the blanks as you listen.

Egypt had one of _________________ civilizations in ancient times. For thousands of years, the Egyptians dominated Northern Africa and parts of the Middle East. The ancient Egyptians _________________ of their civilization. The Great Pyramid of Giza and the Sphinx were the most famous. There were also ruins, statues, and other artifacts all over Egypt. The Egyptians even had _________________. It was called hieroglyphics. It didn't have letters. Instead, it used _________________. But there was a problem: No one could read hieroglyphics. For years, people _________________ various inscriptions. But they didn't succeed.

Then, in 1799, _________________ led by Napoleon invaded Egypt. Some French soldiers went to the city of Rosetta. At Rosetta, they discovered _________________. There was writing in three languages on it. One was hieroglyphics. The other two were ancient Greek and Demotic. The French _________________ the stone.

The French didn't keep the stone for long though. In 1801, British forces defeated the French. They seized the Rosetta Stone and took it to England. In 1802, it _________________ at the British Museum. _________________ they could use the ancient Greek and Demotic inscriptions to understand hieroglyphics. So they studied the Rosetta Stone. It took a long time. But, in 1822, Frenchman Jean Francois Champollion made an announcement. He had translated _________________ in hieroglyphics. _________________, modern-day scholars know _________________ about ancient Egypt since they can read hieroglyphics.

Organizer **Listen to the talk again. Then, fill in the blanks with the correct word(s).**

Ancient Egypt

- Was a great civilization
- Dominated Northern Africa and the Middle ⓐ _________________
- Wrote in the language called ⓑ _________________
- Left many ⓒ _________________ of their civilization

The Rosetta Stone

- Found by French soldiers in ⓓ _________________
- Had writing in hieroglyphics, ancient Greek, and Demotic
- Was translated by Jean Francois Champollion in ⓔ _________________
- Was seized by the ⓕ _________________ and went on display in the British Museum

Main Topic

Circle the correct answer.

1 What is the main idea of the talk?

ⓐ The Rosetta Stone was made during the time of ancient Egypt.

ⓑ The French and British were interested in learning hieroglyphics.

ⓒ The Rosetta Stone helped scholars translate hieroglyphics.

Details

Answer the questions.

2 What did hieroglyphics NOT use?

ⓐ Letters

ⓑ Pictures

ⓒ Symbols

3 Who discovered the Rosetta Stone?

ⓐ Napoleon

ⓑ Some French soldiers

ⓒ British forces

4 What did Jean Francois Champollion do?

ⓐ He translated hieroglyphics.

ⓑ He found the Rosetta Stone.

ⓒ He researched ancient Egyptian ruins.

5 Fill in the blank with the correct word(s).

Because of the Rosetta Stone, scholars can read ________________ today.

Vocabulary

Match the words and phrases with their definitions.

6 go on display ・　　　・ ⓐ to change spoken or written words from one language to another

7 translate ・　　　・ ⓑ to rule over; to be more powerful than

8 dominate ・　　　・ ⓒ words that are written on something like a wall or statue

9 inscription ・　　　・ ⓓ to appear in a museum for people to see

10 seize ・　　　・ ⓔ to take by force

A **Listen to the talk again. Then, put the sentences in chronological order.**

ⓐ __________ Jean Francois Champollion translated the hieroglyphics on the Rosetta Stone.

ⓑ __________ Some French soldiers found the Rosetta Stone.

ⓒ __________ British forces seized the Rosetta Stone from the French.

B **Listen to a news report related to the topic and answer the questions.**

Memo

1 Why did people go to the Library of Alexandria?

ⓐ To meet great scholars

ⓑ To check out books

ⓒ To learn and study

2 What might have happened during Julius Caesar's time?

ⓐ The Library of Alexandria was built.

ⓑ The Library of Alexandria burned down.

ⓒ The city of Alexandria was destroyed.

3 Write the correct time periods in the blanks. Then, put the sentences in chronological order.

ⓐ __________ In the __________________, the city of Alexandria was destroyed.

ⓑ __________ The library burned down in the time of Julius Caesar in the __________________.

ⓒ __________ In __________________, the city of Alexandria was founded.

 11 Penicillin

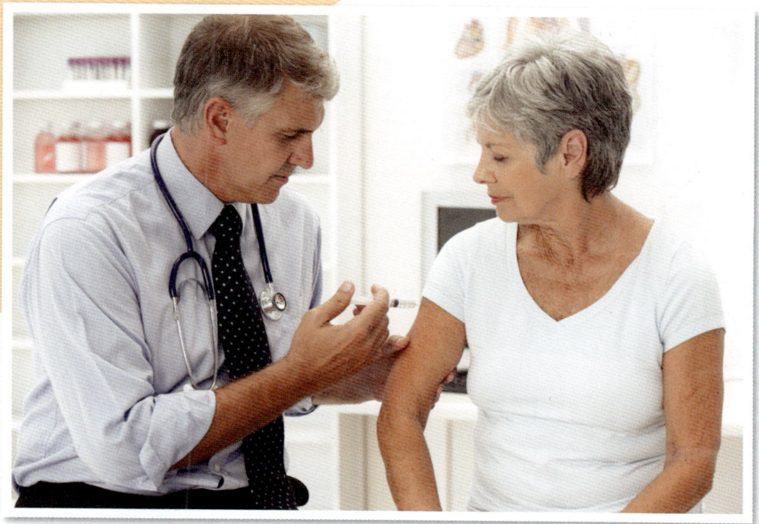

Pre-Listening Questions

Answer the following questions.

1   What is the doctor doing?

2   How does penicillin help people?

3   What are the names of some other medicines? What do they do?

Vocabulary

Look at the pictures. Write the correct word(s) from the box for each picture.

mold	medical researcher	culture dish

1
2
3

Penicillin

Listen to the talk. Fill in the blanks as you listen.

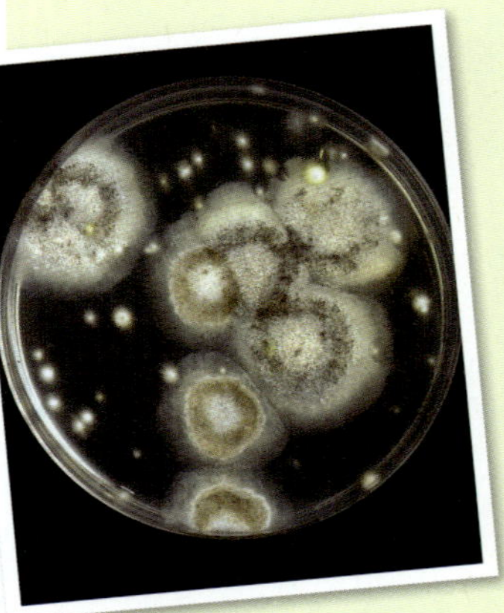

Some of the greatest discoveries in history _____________________.
One of the most vital discoveries of the 1900s happened this way.
Alexander Fleming _____________________. He _____________________.

Alexander Fleming was British. He was born in 1881. He was _____________________. So he studied to be a doctor. He served _____________________ in World War I. It was _____________________. Millions of soldiers died. Often, they died because of _____________________ that they developed after they were wounded.

When the war ended, Fleming became _____________________.
In 1928, he was studying influenza. One day, he made a great discovery. He had been _____________________ in some culture dishes. He noticed that _____________________ was growing in one of the dishes. Fleming looked carefully at the mold. There was _____________________ it that was free of all bacteria. _____________________ all of the bacteria. Fleming realized the importance of this discovery. So he did more research on it. He named the substance he had found penicilin.

Fleming's discovery was important since bacteria _____________________. Doctors had no medicines to cure these infections. As a result, large numbers of their patients died. But pencillin was an antibiotic. Therefore it could _____________________. Fleming wasn't able to turn penicillin into a medicine though. _____________________ did that. Since then, doctors all around the world have used penicillin. It has _____________________ of millions of patients.

Organizer   **Listen to the talk again. Then, fill in the blanks with the correct word(s).**

Circle the correct answer.

1   What is the main topic of the talk?

ⓐ The way penicillin is made

ⓑ The discovery of penicillin

ⓒ The uses of penicillin

Details

Answer the questions.

2   In which war did Alexander Fleming serve as a doctor?

ⓐ World War I

ⓑ World War II

ⓒ The American Civil War

3   What was growing in one of Alexander Fleming's culture dishes?

ⓐ Influenza

ⓑ Mildew

ⓒ Mold

4   Which is NOT true of penicillin?

ⓐ It can kill bacteria.

ⓑ Alexander Fleming turned it into a medicine.

ⓒ It was discovered in 1928.

5   Fill in the blank with the correct word(s).

Penicillin is an important _________________ that was discovered by accident.

Vocabulary

Match the words and phrases with their definitions.

6   germ   •   •   ⓐ without meaning to do something; not on purpose

7   bacterial infection   •   •   ⓑ an invasion of the body by bacteria

8   antibiotic   •   •   ⓒ the flu

9   accidental   •   •   ⓓ a very small organism that can harm people

10 influenza   •   •   ⓔ a type of medicine that is effective against bacteria

A Listen to the talk again.
Then, match each cause with its effect.

ⓐ Because the soldiers had bacterial infections,

ⓑ Fleming knew his discovery was important,

ⓒ Doctors around the world use penicillin,

ⓘ so they have saved many patients' lives.

ⓘⓘ they often died.

ⓘⓘⓘ so he did more research.

B Listen to another talk related to the topic and answer the questions.

1 What did Wilhelm Roentgen do?

ⓐ He discovered X-rays.

ⓑ He took X-rays in hospitals.

ⓒ He made the first cathode ray tube.

2 What did doctors start doing after Wilhelm Roentgen's discovery?

ⓐ Asking Roentgen to build them X-ray machines

ⓑ Taking X-rays in hospitals

ⓒ Learning more about X-rays

3 Circle the correct word in each sentence.

ⓐ (So / Because) Roentgen was doing an experiment, he discovered X-rays.

ⓑ Roentgen experimented with his wife's hand, (so / because) he took an X-ray of it.

ⓒ (So / Because) doctors knew the discovery was important, they took X-rays in hospitals.

The Microwave Oven

Answer the following questions.

1   What is the person doing?

2   How does a microwave oven cook food?

3   What are some advantages of a microwave oven?

Look at the pictures. Write the correct word(s) from the box for each picture.

radar	microwave popcorn	magnetron

1   

2

3

The Microwave Oven

Listen to the talk. Fill in the blanks as you listen.

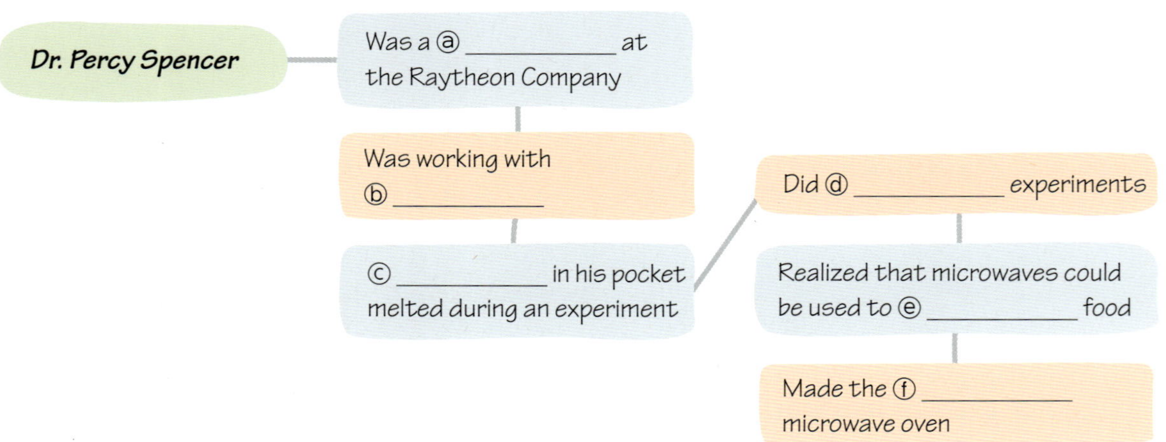

These days, ____________________ have microwave ovens. People use microwaves to do various activities. Microwaves can ____________________. They can defrost food. They can even ____________________. And just like some other ____________________, the technology that the microwave oven uses was discovered ____________________.

In 1946, Dr. Percy Spencer ____________________ the Raytheon Company. He was doing some work with a magnetron. A magnetron was a device that ____________________. It was invented during ____________________. The military used it ____________________.

One day, Dr. Spencer did ____________________ a magnetron. In the middle of the experiment, he ____________________. He remembered that there was a chocolate bar in his pocket. So he reached into his pocket. The chocolate bar was gone though. Instead, there was only ____________________.

Dr. Spencer recognized that the magnetron ____________________ the chocolate. He became curious. So he ____________________. He put some unpopped corn in front of the magnetron. Suddenly, the corn started popping. That was the ____________________. Then, he tried cooking an egg. The egg got hot and ____________________ in one of his colleagues's faces.

Dr. Spencer and Raytheon believed they could build an oven that cooked food with microwaves. So Raytheon made the first microwave oven. It was ____________________. So few people used it. Over time, microwaves got ____________________. Thus more and more people began buying them. Today, they're almost ____________________ refrigerators are in kitchens.

Organizer Listen to the talk again. Then, fill in the blanks with the correct word(s).

Dr. Percy Spencer

Was a ⓐ ____________ at the Raytheon Company

Was working with ⓑ ____________

ⓒ ____________ in his pocket melted during an experiment

Did ⓓ ____________ experiments

Realized that microwaves could be used to ⓔ ____________ food

Made the ⓕ ____________ microwave oven

Circle the correct answer.

1 What is the main idea of the talk?

ⓐ Microwave ovens are convenient appliances in people's kitchens.

ⓑ Dr. Percy Spencer accidentally discovered a new way to cook food.

ⓒ The Raytheon Company made the world's first microwave oven.

Details

Answer the questions.

2 What can a microwave oven NOT do?

ⓐ Defrost food

ⓑ Make ice cream

ⓒ Make popcorn

3 What device melted the chocolate bar in Dr. Percy Spenser's pocket?

ⓐ Radar

ⓑ An oven

ⓒ A magnetron

4 What was the first microwave oven like?

ⓐ Big and expensive

ⓑ Small and fast

ⓒ Big and efficient

5 Fill in the blank with the correct word(s).

The ___________________ made the world's first microwave oven.

Vocabulary

Match the words and phrases with their definitions.

6 melt   •   • ⓐ an improvement; an invention

7 in the middle of   •   • ⓑ to thaw; to removed the ice from

8 innovation   •   • ⓒ to make something change from a solid to a liquid

9 defrost   •   • ⓓ to explode

10 blow up   •   • ⓔ busy; currently doing something

What is cause and effect?

Cause and effect explains why something happens and the result of that action. The cause explains the reason that something occurs. The reason tells the result. The cause and effect may appear in the same sentence or in two different ones. Look carefully to find both of them.

A Listen to the talk again.
Then, match each cause with its effect.

ⓐ The first microwave was big and expensive,

ⓑ The chocolate bar melted,

ⓒ Because Dr. Spencer was curious,

ⓘ so Dr. Spencer realized the magnetron must have done that.

ⓘⓘ so few people used it.

ⓘⓘⓘ he did some more experiments.

B Listen to a student presentation related to the topic and answer the questions.

1 What did Sir Isaac Newton NOT do?

ⓐ He discovered gravity.

ⓑ He invented calculus.

ⓒ He wrote four laws of motion.

2 Why did Sir Isaac Newton think about gravity?

ⓐ An apple hit him in the head.

ⓑ He saw an apple fall to the ground.

ⓒ He watched a man pick an apple from a tree.

3 Circle the correct word in each sentence.

ⓐ Sir Isaac Newton studied many fields of science (so / because) he enjoyed learning.

ⓑ (So / Because) an apple hit him in the head, he discovered gravity.

ⓒ He saw an apple fall from a tree, (so / because) he thought about gravity.

Chapter 4
Great Books

Frankenstein

Pre-Listening Questions

Answer the following questions.

1   How did Dr. Frankenstein make the monster in the picture?

2   What happens in the book *Frankenstein*?

3   What are some other monsters that you know about?

Vocabulary

Look at the pictures. Write the correct word(s) from the box for each picture.

monster	bride	horrified

1   

2   

3   

Frankenstein

Listen to the talk. Fill in the blanks as you listen.

The nineteenth century was a great period for literature. _____________________ many outstanding books then. It was also an _____________________. In the 1800s, people made all kinds of _____________________. So science influenced lots of the works that authors wrote.

One of these authors was Mary Shelley. _____________________, she met with a group of authors. One member of the group was her husband, the poet Percy Shelley. Another was the poet Lord Byron. They all decided to try to write the scariest _____________________. Sometime later, Mary Shelley _____________________. That gave her an idea for a book.

That book became *Frankenstein*. It was one of the greatest books of her time. *Frankenstein* tells the story of Dr. Victor Frankenstein and _____________________ he makes. Frankenstein assembles body parts _____________________. Then, he brings his creation to life. Yet _____________________ the monster.

The rest of the book describes the battle between Frankenstein and the monster. The monster tries to fit in with humans, but _____________________ because of his appearance. He _____________________, so he _____________________ members of Frankenstein's family. He even kills Frankenstein's bride on his wedding night. In the end, Dr. Frankenstein dies. And _____________________.

The book *Frankenstein* was _____________________. It inspired other writers throughout the 1800s. In the 1900s, the story was told _____________________. Today, *Frankenstein* continues to be among _____________________ horror stories of all time.

Organizer **Listen to the talk again. Then, fill in the blanks with the correct word(s).**

Was written by ⓐ _____________ in 1816

Frankenstein

Is about Dr. Frankenstein and his monster

Was in a group of ⓑ _____________

Decided to write the scariest ⓒ _____________ story

Had a ⓓ _____________ that gave her an idea for a book

Assembles body parts from ⓔ _____________ and brings his creation to life

Is ⓕ _____________ by the monster he makes

Circle the correct answer.

1 What is the main topic of the talk?

  ⓐ Why Mary Shelley wrote the book *Frankenstein*

  ⓑ The story of Dr. Frankenstein and his monster

  ⓒ The importance of science in the book *Frankenstein*

Details

Answer the questions.

2 Where did Mary Shelley get the idea for *Frankenstein*?

  ⓐ From Lord Byron

  ⓑ From a dream

  ⓒ From her husband

3 How does Dr. Frankenstein feel about the monster he creates?

  ⓐ He is horrified.

  ⓑ He is amused.

  ⓒ He is satisfied.

4 What does NOT happen in *Frankenstein*?

  ⓐ Dr. Frankenstein builds a monster from dead body parts.

  ⓑ The monster kills Dr. Frankenstein's bride.

  ⓒ Dr. Frankenstein kills the monster.

5 Fill in the blank with the correct word(s).

> Dr. Frankenstein puts together _________________ and then brings the monster to life.

Vocabulary

Match the words and phrases with their definitions.

6 horror story •   • ⓐ to put together

7 fit in with •   • ⓑ a fight

8 assemble •   • ⓒ to belong; to get along with others

9 battle •   • ⓓ a scary story

10 literature •   • ⓔ any kind of writing

What is main idea?

Main idea lets listeners identify the topic of a talk. Listen closely to the information in the talk. Then, decide what the information in the talk is about. The topic of the talk is the main idea. Many times, the speaker will state the main idea in one sentence. This is called the topic sentence.

A Read the following part from the talk. Then, choose the main idea of the talk.

> That book became *Frankenstein*. It was one of the greatest books of her time. *Frankenstein* tells the story of Dr. Victor Frankenstein and the monster he makes. Frankenstein assembles body parts from dead people. Then, he brings his creation to life. Yet he's horrified by his creation.

ⓐ That book became *Frankenstein*.

ⓑ Frankenstein tells the story of Dr. Victor Frankenstein and the monster he makes.

ⓒ Frankenstein assembles body parts from dead people.

B Listen to another talk related to the topic and answer the questions.

1 What kind of book is *Dr. Jekyll and Mr. Hyde*?

ⓐ A biography

ⓑ A science book

ⓒ A novel

2 What does Mr. Hyde do in the story?

ⓐ He works in a laboratory.

ⓑ He commits many crimes.

ⓒ He kills Dr. Jekyll.

3 Listen to the talk again. Then, choose the topic sentence.

ⓐ Robert Louis Stevenson was one of the best writers of the nineteenth century.

ⓑ While Dr. Jekyll is good, Mr. Hyde is bad.

ⓒ *Dr. Jekyll and Mr. Hyde* tells the tale of what happens to both Dr. Jekyll and Mr. Hyde.

Dracula

Answer the following questions.

1   Who was Dracula?

2   What is a vampire?

3   What are a vampire's strengths? What are its weaknesses?

Look at the pictures. Write the correct word(s) from the box for each picture.

sunlight	vampire hunter	stake

1

2

3

Dracula

Listen to the talk. Fill in the blanks as you listen.

There are many ___________________ that people tell. One of the ___________________ ones is the vampire. A vampire appears to be human. But it's actually an undead creature. It survives by ___________________ of humans. A vampire is usually quite strong. It can also often turn itself into a bat. It has few weaknesses. But sunlight can kill a vampire. Stabbing it ___________________ with a wooden stake can kill it. Silver weapons ___________________, too.

Irish writer Bram Stoker did research on the ___________________ about vampires. Then, he wrote the book *Dracula*. He published it in 1897. *Dracula* was a ___________________ that has influenced numerous other works.

In the story, Count Dracula is ___________________ Translyvania. He's also a vampire. Dracula purchases a home in London and makes plans to move there. However, Abraham Van Helsing, a ___________________, discovers him. Van Helsing, along with a small group of men, forces Dracula to leave England and to return to Transylvania. Then, they ___________________ to his home and ___________________ him.

Dracula is one of the ___________________ monsters these days. But the book *Dracula* wasn't ___________________. Instead, it only became ___________________ about it were made. Today, thanks to Bram Stoker's masterpiece, vampire stories are some of the most ___________________ works in the world.

Organizer **Listen to the talk again. Then, fill in the blanks with the correct word(s).**

Vampires

- Are undead creatures that look human
- Drink human ⓐ ___________ and are very strong
- Can be killed by ⓑ ___________, by a wooden stake in the heart, and by silver weapons
- Can turn into a ⓒ ___________

Dracula

- Was written by ⓓ ___________ in 1897
- Tells about the vampire Count ⓔ ___________
- Is a classic horror novel that has ⓕ ___________ many other works
- Is killed by Van Helsing and his small group of men

Main Topic

Circle the correct answer.

1   What is the main idea of the talk?

    ⓐ There are stories about vampires in cultures around the world.

    ⓑ *Dracula* was an outstanding work of horror written by Bram Stoker.

    ⓒ Vampires are dangerous monsters but have a few weaknesses.

Details

Answer the questions.

2   Which is NOT a way to kill a vampire?

    ⓐ By stabbing it in the heart with a wooden stake

    ⓑ By hitting it with silver weapons

    ⓒ By putting some garlic in its mouth

3   Where is Count Dracula from?

    ⓐ Transylvania

    ⓑ London

    ⓒ Pennsylvania

4   What does Abraham Van Helsing do in *Dracula*?

    ⓐ He buys a home in London.

    ⓑ He kills Dracula.

    ⓒ He becomes a vampire.

5   Fill in the blank with the correct word(s).

> *Dracula* was not _________________ at first, but it became a very influential novel in later times.

Vocabulary

Match the words and phrases with their definitions.

6   undead creature   •   • ⓐ a member of a royal family

7   weakness   •   • ⓑ scary

8   purchase   •   • ⓒ to buy

9   noble   •   • ⓓ a fault; a problem; something that is not strong

10 frightening   •   • ⓔ a monster such as a vampire or mummy that is neither living nor dead

A Read the following part from the talk. Then, choose the main idea of the talk.

> Irish writer Bram Stoker did research on the many legends about vampires. Then, he wrote the book *Dracula*. He published it in 1897. *Dracula* was a classic horror novel that has influenced numerous other works.

ⓐ Irish writer Bram Stoker did research on the many legends about vampires.

ⓑ He published it in 1897.

ⓒ *Dracula* was a classic horror novel that has influenced numerous other works.

B Listen to a news report related to the topic and answer the questions.

Memo

1 Where was the gravesite discovered?

ⓐ In England

ⓑ In Poland

ⓒ In Romania

2 Where were the heads of the people in the graves placed?

ⓐ On their legs

ⓑ On the stomachs

ⓒ On their feet

3 Listen to the talk again. Then, choose the topic sentence.

ⓐ Archaeologists recently discovered a gravesite for people believed to be vampires.

ⓑ After the people died, their heads were cut off.

ⓒ Were there really vampires in the past?

Alice's Adventures in Wonderland

Answer the following questions.

1   What can you see in the picture?

2   What do you know about *Alice's Adventures in Wonderland*?

3   Do you know any other fantasy novels? What are they?

Look at the pictures. Write the correct word(s) from the box for each picture.

Cheshire Cat	caterpillar	Mad Hatter

1 

2

3

_______________   _______________   _______________

Alice's Adventures in Wonderland

Listen to the talk. Fill in the blanks as you listen.

One day, a young girl named Alice is sitting with her sister beside a river. She notices ___________________ with clothes on. The rabbit takes out a watch, looks at it, and exclaims, "Oh, dear. I shall ___________________." The rabbit then ___________________ a rabbit hole. Curious, Alice follows the rabbit. She soon falls very far into the hole. Then, she winds up in ___________________ called Wonderland.

That is ___________________ the book *Alice's Adventures in Wonderland*. Lewis Carroll wrote and published it ___________________. Since it was published, it has become one of the most popular ___________________ in the world.

While Alice is in Wonderland, she encounters many strange and ___________________. She meets the white rabbit. She also meets a mouse, a caterpillar, and the Cheshire Cat. In the process, she has a number of odd experiences that ___________________. The Cheshire Cat finally explains to her that everyone in Wonderland is mad. Alice has more adventures after that. She even meets the ___________________ of Wonderland. Finally, at the end of the book, she ___________________ next to her sister. Apparently, she had just been having a dream.

Some of the most ___________________ in literature appear in *Alice's Adventures in Wonderland*. They include the Cheshire Cat, the Mad Hatter, and the ___________________. The book was ___________________ that Carroll wrote a sequel: *Through the Looking Glass*.

Organizer   Listen to the talk again. Then, fill in the blanks with the correct word(s).

Alice's Adventures in Wonderland

- Was written by ⓐ ___________
- Was published in 1865
- Became a popular work of ⓑ ___________
- Sequel is called *Through the Looking Glass*

- Begins when Alice follows a talking ⓒ ___________ down a rabbit hole
- Winds up in ⓓ ___________
- Meets many ⓔ ___________ and wonderful creatures
- Wakes up as she was just having a ⓕ ___________

Main Topic

Circle the correct answer.

1   What is the main idea of the talk?

    ⓐ Alice has many unique adventures while she is in Wonderland.

    ⓑ There are many talking animals that live in Wonderland.

    ⓒ Lewis Carroll wrote the novel *Alice's Adventures in Wonderland*.

Details

Answer the questions.

2   Which creature from Wonderland does Alice see first?

    ⓐ The Mad Hatter

    ⓑ The caterpillar

    ⓒ The white rabbit

3   What does NOT happen to Alice in Wonderland?

    ⓐ She meets the king and queen of Wonderland.

    ⓑ She becomes mad at the Cheshire Cat.

    ⓒ She has a lot of different adventures.

4   What is the title of the sequel to *Alice's Adventures in Wonderland*?

    ⓐ *More Fun with Alice in Wonderland*

    ⓑ *Through the Looking Glass*

    ⓒ *The Return to Wonderland*

5   Fill in the blank with the correct word(s).

> There are many _________________ characters that Alice meets while she is in Wonderland.

Vocabulary

Match the words and phrases with their definitions.

6   wind up   •   • ⓐ to meet

7   encounter   •   • ⓑ a person who is amusing or entertaining

8   colorful character   •   • ⓒ a mirror

9   odd   •   • ⓓ to end up somewhere; to find oneself in a place

10 looking glass   •   • ⓔ strange; weird

A Read the sentences. Then, choose the correct inferences.

ⓐ Alice sees a white rabbit with clothes on. The rabbit can talk. Alice is curious about the rabbit.
  ⓘ Alice wants a pet rabbit.
  ⓘⓘ Alice has never seen a talking rabbit before.

ⓑ Since *Alice's Adventures in Wonderland* was published, it has become a very popular work of fantasy.
  ⓘ Fantasy is the world's most popular genre.
  ⓘⓘ Many people have read *Alice's Adventures in Wonderland*.

ⓒ The Cheshire Cat explains to Alice that everyone in Wonderland is mad.
  ⓘ The Cheshire Cat is mad.
  ⓘⓘ Alice likes the Cheshire Cat.

B Listen to another talk related to the topic and answer the questions.

1 What was George MacDonald's most famous work?
  ⓐ *Phantastes*
  ⓑ *At the Back of the North Wind*
  ⓒ *The Princess and the Goblin*

2 What can be inferred about C.S. Lewis?
  ⓐ He was a better writer than George MacDonald.
  ⓑ He read many of George MacDonald's works.
  ⓒ He and George MacDonald were good friends.

3 What can be inferred about J.R.R. Tolkien?
  ⓐ He was friends with C.S. Lewis.
  ⓑ He wrote works of fantasy.
  ⓒ He was a writer from England.

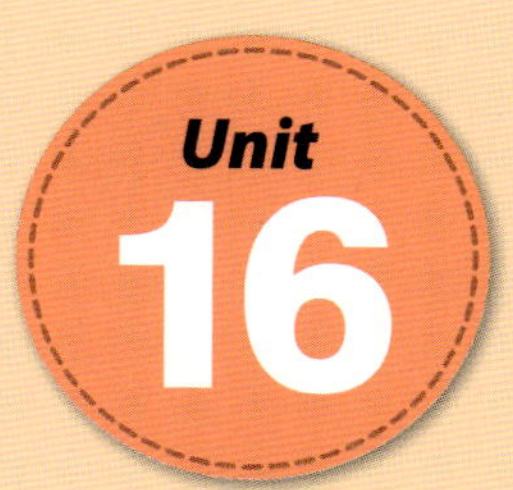

20,000 Leagues under the Sea

Pre-Listening Questions

Answer the following questions.

1   What can you see in the picture?

2   What do you know about *20,000 Leagues under the Sea*?

3   Would you like to ride in a submarine? How do you think it would be?

Vocabulary

Look at the pictures. Write the correct word(s) from the box for each picture.

submarine	Atlantis	beast

1   _______________

2   _______________

3   _______________

20,000 Leagues under the Sea

Listen to the talk. Fill in the blanks as you listen.

Jules Verne was a French author. He lived from 1828 to 1905. Like many other authors from his time, science influenced him ___________________. In fact, people consider him to be the ___________________ fiction. He ___________________ such as *Around the World in 80 Days* and *Journey to the Center of the Earth*. These works—and his others—often focused on the science of ___________________ as well as futuristic science.

His novel *20,000 Leagues under the Sea* ___________________ science. It tells ___________________ Captain Nemo and his submarine the *Nautilus*. Verne published the book in 1869. At that time, there ___________________. They were all primitive. But Verne's submarine was ___________________. It was like the submarines of today.

The story begins with a tale of a beast ___________________. The *Abraham Lincoln*, a ship, sets out to find the beast. It ___________________, which is really the *Nautilus*. During a battle, three of the *Abraham Lincoln*'s crew members fall ___________________. The *Nautilus* rescues them.

The rest of the book describes their time ___________________. The *Nautilus* ___________________ that few men have seen. For instance, it goes to Antarctica. It ___________________ of Atlantis, too.

20,000 Leagues under the Sea is a ___________________. It uses science and technology that didn't exist in Verne's day. However, Verne ___________________ very well. Many of the advances he describes in the book ___________________.

Organizer   **Listen to the talk again. Then, fill in the blanks with the correct word(s).**

Was written by Jules Verne

20,000 Leagues under the Sea

Is the story of Captain Nemo and his ⓓ ___________ the *Nautilus*

Is called the ⓐ ___________ of science fiction

Battles the ship *Abraham Lincoln*

Wrote books such as *Around the World in* ⓑ ___________ and *Journey to the Center of the Earth*

ⓔ ___________ three men who fall into the ocean

Often focused on ⓒ ___________ science

Visits places such as ⓕ ___________ and the ruins of Atlantis

Main Topic

Circle the correct answer.

1 What is the main topic of the talk?

   ⓐ Why Jules Verne wrote *20,000 Leagues under the Sea*

   ⓑ The science-fiction novels that Jules Verne wrote

   ⓒ The events in *20,000 Leagues under the Sea*

Details

Answer the questions.

2 Which of the following is NOT true about Jules Verne?

   ⓐ People call him the father of science fiction.

   ⓑ He sometimes wrote works of fantasy.

   ⓒ He used a lot of science in his novels.

3 Who is Captain Nemo?

   ⓐ The captain of the *Nautilus*

   ⓑ The captain of the *Abraham Lincoln*

   ⓒ The captain of the *Enterprise*

4 Where does the *Nautilus* visit in *20,000 Leagues under the Sea*?

   ⓐ The North Pole

   ⓑ The Gulf of Mexico

   ⓒ The ruins of Atlantis

5 Fill in the blank with the correct word(s).

   20,000 Leagues under the Sea is a _________________ adventure novel that uses futuristic science.

Vocabulary

Match the words and phrases with their definitions.

6 thrilling   •   • ⓐ very much; a lot

7 a great deal   •   • ⓑ relating to or concerning the future

8 futuristic   •   • ⓒ to depart; to start going somewhere

9 primitive   •   • ⓓ exciting

10 set out   •   • ⓔ basic; simple

A Read the sentences. Then, choose the correct inferences.

ⓐ Jules Verne wrote *Around the World in 80 Days* and *Journey to the Center of the Earth*. These works often focused on the science of his time as well as futuristic science.
　ⓘ *Journey to the Center of the Earth* is a work of science fiction.
　ⓘⓘ Most of Jules Verne's novels were popular with readers.

ⓑ During Verne's time, there were only a few primitive submarines. But the *Nautilus* was very advanced.
　ⓘ Verne was the first person to build an advanced submarine.
　ⓘⓘ There were no submarines like the *Nautilus* during Verne's lifetime.

ⓒ The book describes some adventures under the sea. The *Nautilus* visits the ruins of Atlantis.
　ⓘ The ruins of Atlantis are under water.
　ⓘⓘ Atlantis was once a great civilization.

B Listen to a school report related to the topic and answer the questions.

1 What can be inferred about the speaker?

　ⓐ He likes *Paris in the Twentieth Century*.

　ⓑ He does not enjoy books by Jules Verne.

　ⓒ He wants to live in a future society.

2 Why did it take a long time to publish *Paris in the Twentieth Century*?

　ⓐ It took Verne a long time to write it.

　ⓑ The manuscript got lost.

　ⓒ Jules Verne did not like the book.

3 What can be inferred about life in Jules Verne's time?

　ⓐ Most people traveled by train.

　ⓑ There were no tall skyscrapers made of glass.

　ⓒ It resembled the modern world of the 1900s.

The Koala

Answer the following questions.

1   Where does the koala live?

2   What kind of animal is the koala?

3   What else do you know about the koala?

Look at the pictures. Write the correct word(s) from the box for each picture.

fur	eucalyptus tree	poisonous

1   ____________________

2   ____________________

3   ____________________

The Koala

Listen to the talk. Fill in the blanks as you listen.

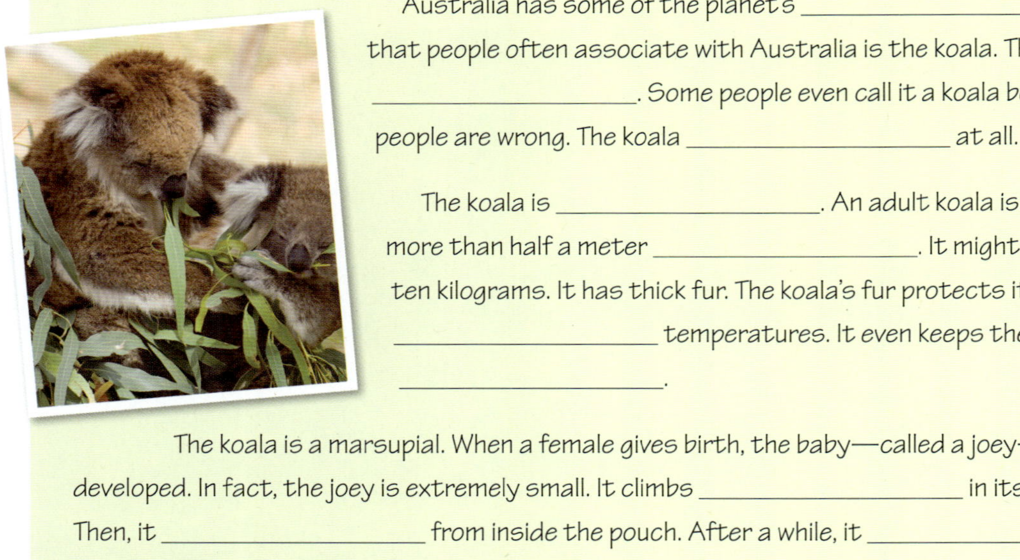

Australia has some of the planet's _____________________. One animal that people often associate with Australia is the koala. The koala looks _____________________. Some people even call it a koala bear. But these people are wrong. The koala _____________________ at all.

The koala is _____________________. An adult koala is usually a little more than half a meter _____________________. It might weigh around ten kilograms. It has thick fur. The koala's fur protects it from both _____________________ temperatures. It even keeps the koala dry _____________________.

The koala is a marsupial. When a female gives birth, the baby—called a joey—isn't fully developed. In fact, the joey is extremely small. It climbs _____________________ in its mother's body. Then, it _____________________ from inside the pouch. After a while, it _____________________. At that time, it can survive outside its mother's pouch.

The koala spends most of its _____________________. It likes the eucalyptus tree in particular. The koala mainly eats the leaves of that tree. This is unique because eucalyptus _____________________ to most other animals. But the koala can eat the leaves _____________________ any problems.

Unfortunately, there are _____________________ eucalyptus trees in Australia these days. The reason is that people are _____________________. As a result, there are only around 100,000 koalas in Australia today. And the number of koalas _____________________ even more in the future.

Organizer **Listen to the talk again. Then, fill in the blanks with the correct word(s).**

The Koala			
Is half a meter in length and ⓐ _____________ kilograms	Has ⓑ _____________ fur that protects it from heat and cold		
Is a marsupial	Gives birth to ⓒ _____________ called joeys	Babies crawl into ⓓ _____________ and develop more from there	
Lives most of its life in ⓔ _____________	Eats the leaves of the ⓕ _____________ tree	Are fewer eucalyptus trees, so its numbers are declining	

Main Topic

Circle the correct answer.

1 What is the main idea of the talk?

ⓐ The koala is a marsupial that lives in Australia.

ⓑ There are not many koalas alive today.

ⓒ The koala eats the leaves of the eucalyptus tree.

Details

Answer the questions.

2 Which is NOT true about the koala?

ⓐ It lives in Australia.

ⓑ It is a bear.

ⓒ It weighs around ten kilograms.

3 What does a joey do when it is born?

ⓐ It climbs onto its mother's back.

ⓑ It climbs onto its mother's tail.

ⓒ It climbs into its mother's pouch.

4 What does the koala eat?

ⓐ The leaves of the eucalyptus tree

ⓑ The fruit of the eucalyptus tree

ⓒ The flower of the eucalyptus tree

5 Fill in the blank with the correct word(s).

> The number of koalas is _________________ because people are chopping down many eucalyptus trees.

Vocabulary

Match the words and phrases with their definitions.

6 suffer •   • ⓐ a pocket

7 extremely •   • ⓑ an animal like a mammal but which has a pouch that its babies live in

8 pouch •   • ⓒ very

9 chop down •   • ⓓ to experience pain or a problem

10 marsupial •   • ⓔ to cut down something such as a tree

What is summarizing?
Summarizing can help you determine the main point of a talk. To summarize a talk, forget about the minor details and unimportant information. Think about the most important ideas and details in the talk. Then, try to put them into one sentence. This is the summary sentence.

A **Listen to the talk again. Then, choose the correct summary sentence.**

ⓐ Many people think that the koala is a bear, but that is not true about the animal.

ⓑ It is important to take care of the koala because there are only 100,000 left.

ⓒ The koala is an Australian marsupial that eats the leaves of the eucalyptus tree.

B **Listen to another talk related to the topic and answer the questions.**

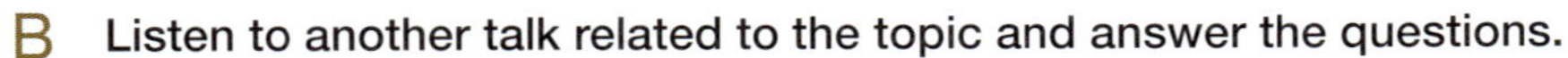

> **NOTE**

1 What are the feet of the duck-billed platypus like?

ⓐ The feet of an otter

ⓑ The feet of a duck

ⓒ The feet of a beaver

2 Where are the duck-billed platypus's stingers?

ⓐ On its back feet

ⓑ On its back

ⓒ On its tail

3 Choose the correct summary sentence.

ⓐ The duck-billed platypus can swim in water and also walk on land.

ⓑ The duck-billed platypus has several characteristics that make it very unusual.

ⓒ The duck-billed platypus is a mammal that lives in parts of Australia.

18 The Komodo Dragon

Pre-Listening Questions

Answer the following questions.

1. What kind of animal is the Komodo dragon?

2. Where do you think it lives?

3. What kind of animal does it remind you of?

Vocabulary

Look at the pictures. Write the correct word(s) from the box for each picture.

prehistoric animal	lizard	breathe fire

1

2

3

The Komodo Dragon

Listen to the talk. Fill in the blanks as you listen.

Dinosaurs once lived all over the planet. They died around ___________________ years ago though. Today, there aren't any dinosaurs anywhere. There are, however, some creatures that remind people of ___________________. One of these creatures is the Komodo dragon. It lives on ___________________ in Indonesia.

The Komodo dragon isn't like a mythical dragon. It doesn't have wings. And it ___________________ or speak either. Yet it's still ___________________. The Komodo dragon is the world's ___________________. It can grow longer than three meters ___________________ of its nose to the end of its tail. The average Komodo dragon weighs ___________________ kilograms. But the largest one ever caught weighed 166 kilograms.

The Komodo dragon ___________________ for a couple of reasons. First, most lizards are omnivores. So they eat both ___________________ matter. The Komodo dragon, on the other hand, is a carnivore. It ___________________. And, due to its great size, it needs lots of meat. It eats all kinds of small animals. But it also hunts and ___________________, wild pigs, deer, and other animals of similar sizes. It even hunts humans ___________________.

The lizard ___________________ when it attacks. It often doesn't kill its prey with the first bite. But its saliva has ___________________ of bacteria. The bacteria kill any animal the Komodo dragon bites after ___________________. So it simply ___________________ until it dies. Then, it has a meal.

Organizer Listen to the talk again. Then, fill in the blanks with the correct word(s).

Lives on some islands in
ⓐ ___________

The Komodo Dragon

Is a carnivore so only eats
ⓓ ___________

Is the world's
ⓑ ___________ lizard

Can be three meters long and weighs around
ⓒ ___________ kilograms

ⓔ ___________ both small and big animals

ⓕ ___________ animals and then lets the bacteria in its saliva kills its prey

Main Topic

Circle the correct answer.

1   What is the main topic of the talk?

ⓐ The place where the Komodo dragon lives

ⓑ The characteristics of the Komodo dragon

ⓒ The life cycle of the Komodo dragon

Details

Answer the questions.

2   What does the Komodo dragon remind people of?

ⓐ Dinosaurs

ⓑ Turtles

ⓒ Snakes

3   Which statement about the Komodo dragon is true?

ⓐ It has an average weight of 166 kilograms.

ⓑ Its tail can be more than three meters long.

ⓒ It hunts large animals such as deer and pigs.

4   Which of the following does the Komodo dragon NOT do when it hunts animals?

ⓐ It lets bacteria in its saliva kill animals.

ⓑ It bites the animals it attacks.

ⓒ It uses its claws to attack some animals.

5   Fill in the blank with the correct word(s).

The Komodo dragon is not an omnivore like most lizards but is instead a ______________.

Vocabulary

Match the words with their definitions.

6   creature   •   • ⓐ amazing; remarkable

7   omnivore   •   • ⓑ an animal

8   impressive •   • ⓒ legendary; fabulous

9   saliva   •   • ⓓ spit

10 mythical   •   • ⓔ an animal that eats both meat and vegetation

A   **Listen to the talk again. Then, choose the correct summary sentence.**

ⓐ The Komodo dragon is a large carnivorous lizard that lives on some islands in Indonesia.

ⓑ Because the Komodo dragon is so big, it can hunt animals that are very large.

ⓒ The bite of the Komodo dragon is deadly to most animals.

B   **Listen to a talk by a zookeeper related to the topic and answer the questions.**

1   Where does the green basilisk lizard live?

ⓐ In rainforests

ⓑ Near rivers

ⓒ By the sea

2   What can the green basilisk lizard do?

ⓐ It can swim in the water.

ⓑ It can run on the water.

ⓒ It can catch fish in the water.

3   Choose the correct summary sentence.

ⓐ The green basilisk lizard lives in the rainforests of Central and South America.

ⓑ The zoo has a green basilisk lizard in one of its exhibits.

ⓒ The green basilisk lizard is an animal that can run on the surface of the water.

The Walking Leaf

Pre-Listening Questions

Pre-Listening Questions

Answer the following questions.

1   What kind of animal is the walking leaf?

2   Can you find the walking leaf in the picture on the right?

3   Do you know some other animals that use camouflage?

Vocabulary

Look at the pictures. Write the correct word(s) from the box for each picture.

zebra	camouflage	walking stick

1

2

3

The Walking Leaf

Listen to the talk. Fill in the blanks as you listen.

A lot of animals use camoflauge. This means that they ______________________ other animals. Animals use camouflage ______________________. The easiest way is the color of the animal. Look at many forest animals. Animals like rabbits and deer are often brown. This helps them ______________________ the color of the ground. Animals like ______________________ have stripes. Their stripes are forms of camouflage as well.

A few animals use ______________________. They resemble various inanimate objects. For example, the rockfish resembles a rock. The ______________________ looks like a stick from a tree or bush. And the walking leaf resembles ______________________ of a tree.

The walking leaf is an insect. It lives mostly ______________________ and Australia. It lives in various ecosystems. But it's somewhat ______________________. The walking leaf is ______________________ because it really looks like a leaf. Sometimes parts of a walking leaf's body even appear to have ______________________ on it. That provides even more camouflage for it.

The walking leaf uses its ______________________ to hide from predators. Many animals simply don't notice the walking leaf even if they're next to it. When the walking leaf moves, its body sways from ______________________. This makes it appear as if the ______________________ the leaf. It's a very effective disguise for the insect. And it helps prevent predators ______________________ and eating it.

Organizer Listen to the talk again. Then, fill in the blanks with the correct word(s).

Camouflage

- Is a way to ⓐ ______________ from other animals
- Can be color of animal or ⓑ ______________
- Rockfish looks like a ⓒ ______________, and walking stick looks like a stick
- Some animals look like inanimate objects

The Walking Leaf

- Resembles the ⓓ ______________ of a tree
- Lives in ⓔ ______________ in Asia and Australia
- Moves back and forth when it walks so that it looks like the ⓕ ______________ is blowing a leaf
- Is able to hide from predators because of its body

Circle the correct answer.

1   What is the main topic of the talk?

    ⓐ The best ways to use camouflage

    ⓑ Different animals that use camouflage

    ⓒ How the walking leaf uses camouflage

Details

Answer the questions.

2   Which animal does NOT use camouflage?

    ⓐ The deer

    ⓑ The eagle

    ⓒ The tiger

3   What is true about the walking leaf's body?

    ⓐ It is both green and brown in color.

    ⓑ It can be up to eight centimeters long.

    ⓒ It sometimes appears to have bite marks.

4   How does the walking leaf's body help it?

    ⓐ It can avoid predators.

    ⓑ It can hunt other insects well.

    ⓒ It can climb trees easily.

5   Fill in the blank with the correct word(s).

> The walking leaf looks like the leaf of a tree, so it uses a form of ___________________.

Vocabulary

Match the words and phrases with their definitions.

6   sway •   • ⓐ to look like

7   resemble •   • ⓑ very interesting; amazing

8   disguise •   • ⓒ anything that is not alive

9   inanimate object •   • ⓓ a way of making something look different than normal

10 fascinating •   • ⓔ to move back and forth

Listening Skills Practice: Word Stress I

A Listen to the talk again. Then, circle the words that the speaker stresses.

ⓐ The easiest way is the color of the animal.

ⓑ The walking leaf is a fascinating insect because it really looks like a leaf.

ⓒ That provides even more camouflage for it.

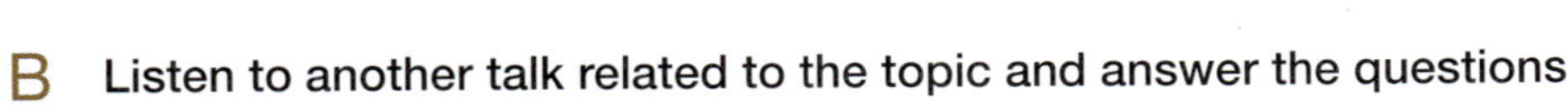

B Listen to another talk related to the topic and answer the questions.

NOTE

1 What kind of animal is the praying mantis?

ⓐ An insect

ⓑ A mammal

ⓒ A reptile

2 Which of the following does the praying mantis NOT hunt?

ⓐ Birds

ⓑ Insects

ⓒ Fish

3 Listen to the talk again. Then, circle the words that the speaker stresses.

ⓐ But it does not use camouflage for defensive purposes.

ⓑ They can be more than fifteen centimeters long.

ⓒ Now that's impressive.

The Hummingbird

Answer the following questions.

1   What does the hummingbird usually eat?

2   How big is the hummingbird?

3   What else do you know about the hummingbird?

Look at the pictures. Write the correct word(s) from the box for each picture.

backward	helicopter	upside down

1   

2

3

_________________   _________________   _________________

The Hummingbird

Listen to the talk. Fill in the blanks as you listen.

Every spring and summer, there's a common sight in many flower gardens. It's the tiny hummingbird flying from ___________________.

It does this to drink nectar from flowers. Many people who watch the hummingbird notice one unusual thing about it: It ___________________ but continues to flap its wings as it feeds. However, it doesn't move as it flies. Instead, it hovers ___________________.

The hummingbird is unusual for many reasons. First, it's the ___________________ birds. A typical adult hummingbird is around eight centimeters long. It also weighs between only two and twenty grams. But the ___________________ about this bird concerns ___________________. Like all birds, the hummingbird can fly forward. But, unlike all other birds, the hummingbird can fly backward. It can also fly from ___________________ the left or right. It can hover in the air. Finally, it can even fly upside down. ___________________ are capable of such aerial feats.

The hummingbird can fly like this thanks to ___________________. Its wings can rotate completely ___________________. That lets it fly in so many directions. In addition, the hummingbird flaps its wings very swiftly. While flying, it flaps its wings around eighty times ___________________. In some instances, it can flap its wings more than 200 times a second. That's ___________________. In fact, it's so fast that the bird's wings make ___________________. That's why it's called the hummingbird.

Organizer   **Listen to the talk again. Then, fill in the blanks with the correct word(s).**

Is the ⓐ ___________ bird in the world

The Hummingbird

Can fly forward, ⓓ ___________, from side to side, and upside down

ⓑ ___________ is around eight centimeters long

Can hover in the air like a helicopter

Weighs between ⓒ ___________ and twenty grams

Can fly like that because its wings can ⓔ ___________ completely in a circle

Flaps its wings ⓕ ___________ times per second while flying

Main Topic

Circle the correct answer.

1 What is the main idea of the talk?

ⓐ The hummingbird is unique because of its flying ability.

ⓑ The smallest bird in the world is the hummingbird.

ⓒ The hummingbird likes to eat nectar from flowers.

Details

Answer the questions.

2 What does the hummingbird do while it feeds from flowers?

ⓐ It hovers in the air.

ⓑ It flies upside down.

ⓒ It moves from left to right.

3 Which of the following is NOT true about the hummingbird?

ⓐ It is the smallest bird in the world.

ⓑ An adult is around eight centimeters long.

ⓒ It weighs between 2 and 20 kilograms.

4 How fast does a hummingbird flap its wings while it is flying?

ⓐ 20 times a second

ⓑ 50 times a second

ⓒ 80 times a second

5 Fill in the blank with the correct word(s).

A hummingbird flaps its wings so fast that they make a _________________ sound.

Vocabulary

Match the words and phrases with their definitions.

6 nectar • • ⓐ to be flying in the air but not moving anywhere

7 aerial feat • • ⓑ to move around in a circle

8 flap one's wings • • ⓒ to move one's wings back and forth in order to fly

9 hover • • ⓓ a sweet substance made by flowers

10 rotate • • ⓔ a trick that one does while flying

Listening Skills Practice: Word Stress II

A   **Listen to the talk again. Then, circle the words that the speaker stresses.**

ⓐ It does not land but continues to flap its wings as it feeds.

ⓑ But, unlike all other birds, the hummingbird can fly backward.

ⓒ In addition, the hummingbird flaps its wings very swiftly.

B   **Listen to another talk related to the topic and answer the questions.**

1   What do people often say about bats?

ⓐ They like to bite humans.

ⓑ They are blind.

ⓒ They are poor at flying.

2   How do bats use echolocation?

ⓐ By making very high-pitched sounds

ⓑ By using their eyes like radar

ⓒ By closely observing the objects around them

3   Listen to the talk again. Then, circle the words that the speaker stresses.

ⓐ I think you're going to have a great time.

ⓑ Bats have poor eyesight, but they can still see.

ⓒ And it also makes them really unusual creatures.

Answers

Chapter 1 Astronomy

Unit 01 Asteroids and Comets

p. 11

Pre-Listening Questions `Sample Answer`

1 It looks like an asteroid. I think it's going to hit the Earth.
2 They are both small objects in outer space. I think asteroids are like big rocks. And comets have long tails.
3 Yes, they can. Sometimes they hit the Earth. They can cause lots of damage.

Vocabulary

1 tail
2 asteroid
3 dinosaur

p. 12

Script

M Teacher: There are many objects in the solar system. The biggest is the sun. The planets orbit the sun. And the moons go around their planets. There are many other objects that also orbit the sun. Some of the most common are asteroids and comets.

Asteroids are pieces of rock that orbit the sun. They're often made of metal. Iron and nickel are common metals in asteroids. Asteroids vary in size. Some are just small rocks. Others are quite large. Ceres is the biggest asteroid in the solar system. It's about 900 kilometers in diameter. Most asteroids orbit the sun in the asteroid belt. It's located between Mars and Jupiter.

Comets are different from asteroids. They're made of ice, dust, and small rocks. They also orbit the sun. But they usually take decades or even hundreds of years to complete one orbit. Comets sometimes get very bright. This happens when they go near the sun. The sun melts some of their ice. So the comets get long tails. Occasionally, we can see bright comets from the Earth. Some comets have tails so long that they can cover much of the sky.

Are asteroids and comets dangerous? They can be. In the past, both have hit the Earth. Scientists believe a big asteroid hit the Earth and killed the dinosaurs millions of years ago. Today, astronomers watch the skies for asteroids and comets. They don't want another one to hit the Earth today. That could kill millions of people.

Organizer

ⓐ sun
ⓑ iron
ⓒ Mars
ⓓ ice
ⓔ orbit
ⓕ bright

p. 13

Comprehension

1 ⓑ
2 ⓐ
3 ⓑ
4 ⓑ
5 dinosaurs
6 ⓒ
7 ⓔ
8 ⓐ
9 ⓑ
10 ⓓ

p. 14

Listening Skills Practice: Compare and Contrast I

A ⓐ contrast
  ⓑ compare
  ⓒ contrast

B

Script

W Teacher: Sometimes at night, you may see a bright light flash across the sky. We call that light a shooting star. But it's not really a star. It's a meteor. We actually use three words. They are meteoroid, meteor, and meteorite. Let me tell you the difference between them. Any small object in outer space that isn't an asteroid or a comet is a meteoroid. Meteoroids are very small. They can be small rocks or tiny grains of sand. Sometimes meteoroids enter the Earth's atmosphere. Then, we call them meteors. A shooting star you see at night is really just a meteor. It's burning up in the air. Most meteors completely burn up in the atmosphere. Some don't. If a meteor lands on the ground, we call it a meteorite. A meteorite is usually a small chunk of rock.

1 ⓒ
2 ⓐ
3 ⓐ ⓘ   ⓑ ⓘ   ⓒ ⓘⓘⓘ

Eclipses

p. 15

Pre-Listening Questions Sample Answer

1 They are the sun and the moon. The moon is in front of the sun.
2 An object like the moon gets between the sun and Earth.
3 No, I haven't. I would like to see an eclipse though.

Vocabulary

1 revolve
2 blocked
3 solar system

p. 16

Script

M Teacher: The objects in the solar system are in constant motion. For example, Earth moves around the sun. The other planets move around the sun, too. The moons move around various planets. For example, Earth's moon revolves around Earth. Sometimes two objects in space form a line with the sun. When this happens, there's an eclipse.

There are two kinds of eclipses. There are solar eclipses and lunar eclipses. A solar eclipse happens when the moon moves between the sun and Earth. However, a lunar eclipse happens when Earth moves between the moon and the sun. These two kinds of eclipses have different results.

For instance, solar eclipses are very rare. But lunar eclipses are more common. In addition, solar eclipses last for a short amount of time. They usually only last for a few minutes. They can also only be seen in certain places on the planet. On the other hand, lunar eclipses can last for a longer period of time. They may last for an hour and a half. Solar eclipses are more impressive than lunar eclipses though. During a lunar eclipse, the moon may change colors. It may look like it is red. During a solar eclipse, the sun's light is blocked. So it becomes dark during the day. Solar eclipses can be dangerous. People shouldn't look directly at them. But it's okay to look straight at a lunar eclipse.

Organizer

ⓐ moon ⓑ dark
ⓒ dangerous ⓓ between
ⓔ common ⓕ red

p. 17

Comprehension

1	ⓑ	2	ⓐ	3	ⓐ
4	ⓑ	5	solar		
6	ⓔ	7	ⓒ	8	ⓑ
9	ⓓ	10	ⓐ		

p. 18

Listening Skills Practice: Compare and Contrast II

A ⓐ but
   ⓑ Both
   ⓒ and

B

Script

M News Broadcaster: Good evening, everyone. This is Keith Roberts with the evening news. I want to remind you all about the solar eclipse tomorrow. It's going to start at ten twenty-two in the morning. And it's going to last for around five minutes. We're very lucky since this is going to be a total eclipse of the sun. There are two kinds of eclipses. There are total and partial eclipses. In a partial eclipse, only a small part of the sun is blocked. But we're getting a total eclipse. So the moon will block nearly all of the sun's light. Don't look straight at either kind of solar eclipse though. It could damage your eyes. You might even go blind. Here's Dana Walton. She'll tell you a safe way to look at the eclipse.

1 ⓐ
2 ⓒ
3 ⓐ however
   ⓑ Both
   ⓒ and

p. 19

Pre-Listening Questions `Sample Answer`

1   He was an astronomer. He lived a long time ago.
2   I can see a planet with four small objects around it. Maybe they are moons.
3   I think each moon orbits its planet.

Vocabulary

1   mathematician
2   telescope
3   tutor

p. 20

Script

W Teacher: Galileo Galilei was born in Pisa, Italy, in 1564. He lived during the Renaissance. This was a time of <u>great learning</u> in Europe. Education was very important then. So Galileo's father <u>hired a tutor</u> for him. Galileo studied hard and learned a lot. He had <u>many interests in</u> his life. He was an astronomer, mathematician, inventor, and physicist. But most people today <u>remember him for</u> his work in astronomy.

Galileo was really interested <u>in the stars</u>. He wanted to <u>look closely at</u> them. He heard about <u>a new invention</u>: eyeglasses. Galileo decided to make his own. The result was <u>the first telescope</u>. Galileo used his new invention to look at the night sky. Thanks to it, he could see objects <u>very close up</u>.

Galileo looked at the moon. He saw many of its craters. Then, he looked at Jupiter. He saw four tiny objects around it. These were Jupiter's <u>four biggest moons</u>. Today, they are called the Galilean moons. More notably, Galileo realized that they were <u>going around Jupiter</u>. In the past, people believed that everything in the sky—the sun, stars, moon, and planets—orbited Earth. This was called the geocentric model of the universe. Galileo realized that <u>it was wrong</u>. He believed in a new theory. It was called the heliocentric model of the universe. It stated that the objects in the solar system <u>orbit the sun</u>, not Earth. Many people <u>disagreed with</u> Galileo. But this model of the universe was correct.

Organizer

ⓐ astronomer
ⓒ night
ⓔ moons
ⓑ telescope
ⓓ Jupiter
ⓕ heliocentric

p. 21

Comprehension

1   ⓒ   2   ⓑ   3   ⓐ
4   ⓒ   5   Jupiter

6   ⓒ   7   ⓔ   8   ⓓ
9   ⓐ   10 ⓑ

p. 22

Listening Skills Practice: Outlining I

A   ⓐ Renaissance
    ⓑ inventor
    ⓒ Discovered
    ⓓ orbited
    ⓔ geocentric

B

Script

W Teacher: We use telescopes to look closely at objects in the night sky. There are many kinds of telescopes. But most people use two types. They are refracting and reflecting telescopes. They're both a little different from each other. Galileo Galilei made the first telescope. It was a refracting one. His invention used lenses to make distant objects appear closer. Refracting telescopes are great for looking at nearby objects such as planets. They are also good for observing bright stars. But they can cost a lot of money. Most people believe that Sir Isaac Newton made the first reflecting telescope. These telescopes use mirrors to collect light. That lets them observe objects. They are great for looking at very distant objects. They don't cost a lot of money either. Reflecting telescopes are also often bigger than refracting ones.

1   ⓐ Refracting
    ⓑ lenses
    ⓒ nearby
    ⓓ mirrors
    ⓔ distant
    ⓕ money
2   ⓒ

Percival Lowell

p. 23

Pre-Listening Questions `Sample Answer`

1 It looks like a desert in the first picture. The second picture is a planet. But I don't know the name of the planet.
2 They are Mercury, Venus, Earth, Mars, Jupiter, Saturn, Uranus, and Neptune.
3 I'm not sure. I hope so. I think that would be exciting.

Vocabulary

1 canal
2 Mars
3 orbit

p. 24

Script

M Teacher: In the 1800s, there were <u>numerous scientific advances</u>. They made many people <u>become interested in</u> science. One of those people was Percival Lowell. He was born <u>in 1855</u> and died in 1916. Lowell focused much of his life on astronomy. Today, people remember him for two things: <u>Mars and Pluto</u>.

In the 1800s, people were fascinated with Mars. They often <u>wondered if</u> there was life on that planet. There were lots of books and stories about Mars in popular culture. *The War of the Worlds* by H.G. Wells was the most famous one. Lowell spent more than fifteen years studying Mars. He <u>looked closely at</u> it with telescopes. He <u>saw lines</u> on the planet. Lowell thought <u>they were canals</u>. So he believed there was <u>life on Mars</u>. He even wrote a couple of books about Mars. They were very popular with the reading public. Unfortunately, there was no life on Mars. So Lowell <u>was wrong about</u> that.

He wasn't, however, wrong about Pluto. For centuries, people knew about <u>five planets</u>. They knew about Mercury, Venus, Mars, Jupiter, and Saturn. Then, in 1781, Uranus was discovered. In 1846, Neptune was located. Lowell studied the orbits of both planets. He thought that the gravity of <u>an unknown planet</u> was affecting them. He called it Planet X. In 1906, Lowell <u>started looking for</u> Planet X. He continued his search until he died. He never found it. But others kept searching. In 1930, Clyde Tombaugh <u>discovered Planet X</u>. It was <u>later named</u> Pluto.

Organizer

ⓐ Mars
ⓑ fifteen
ⓒ canals
ⓓ Uranus
ⓔ affecting
ⓕ Pluto

p. 25

Comprehension

1 ⓑ
2 ⓑ
3 ⓒ
4 ⓐ
5 Pluto
6 ⓐ
7 ⓑ
8 ⓔ
9 ⓒ
10 ⓓ

p. 26

Listening Skills Practice: Outlining II

A ⓐ Mars
   ⓑ canals
   ⓒ solar system
   ⓓ Planet X
   ⓔ Clyde Tombaugh

B

Script

M Announcer: Thank you for coming to tonight's special debate at Central Library. This evening, the topic of our debate is Mars. We specifically want to know the answer to this question: Was there ever life on Mars? We've got two local astronomers here to talk about the issue. The first is Professor Mark Chapman from Western University. He believes that there used to be life on Mars. However, he claims that there is not any life on the planet now. According to him, it died a long time ago. The second astronomer is Professor Susan Perkins. She teaches at Chase College. Professor Perkins believes there has never been life on Mars. In fact, she thinks that the only life in the universe is on Earth. It's time to begin the debate. Let's start with Professor Chapman. Please give your opening statement, sir.

1 ⓐ life
   ⓑ past
   ⓒ died
   ⓓ never
   ⓔ universe
2 ⓑ

Chapter 2 Norse Mythology

Unit 05 Norse Gods and Goddesses

p. 29

Pre-Listening Questions Sample Answer

1   I think that's Odin on the left. I'm not sure about the goddess. And that might be Thor in the third picture.

2   There are lots of stories about fighting. Thor is in many of the stories. And there are giants in some Norse myths.

3   I know an old Korean story. Once, a bear and a tiger wanted to become humans. They were told by Hwanwoong, a god, that they could become humans if they only ate garlic and onions in the dark for 100 days. Only the patient bear became a human. It married Hwanwoong. Then, they had a son named Dangun.

Vocabulary

1   Scandinavia
2   warrior
3   battle

p. 30

Script

W Teacher: Many people _are familiar with_ the Greek gods and goddesses. A lot of people know about the Roman gods and goddesses, too. But _fewer know about_ the Norse gods and goddesses. Norse mythology _comes from_ Scandinavia. Denmark, Norway, Sweden, and Finland are all in Scandinavia.

There were many gods and goddesses in Norse mythology. Odin was one of them. Odin was the father of all _gods and men_. He was a very wise god. He only had _one eye_. He often had two ravens with him. Their names were Hugin and Munin. Another well-known god was Thor. Thor was the strongest and _most powerful_ of the Norse gods. He protected Midgard. It was the land where humans lived. He carried _a large hammer_ and was known as the Thunderer. Loki was another god. He was the trickster god. In many Norse myths, Loki caused a lot of the problems the gods _had to solve_. Some other Norse gods were Tyr, Freyr, and Heimdall.

Goddesses were also important in Norse mythology. Freya was the goddess of love and beauty. But she was also _a warrior goddess_. Frigga was Odin's wife and was

the _protector of children_. Skadi was the goddess of winter. Hel was the goddess of _the underworld_.

There were many other gods and goddesses in Norse mythology. They often _battled the giants_ and other monsters. Their stories are often _very entertaining_.

Organizer

ⓐ father   ⓑ Thor
ⓒ trickster   ⓓ love
ⓔ wife   ⓕ winter

p. 31

Comprehension

1   ⓑ   2   ⓒ   3   ⓐ
4   ⓑ   5   Scandinavia

6   ⓑ   7   ⓓ   8   ⓔ
9   ⓒ   10   ⓐ

p. 32

Listening Skills Practice: Note-Taking I

A

ⓐ Norse mythology comes from Scandinavia. Denmark, Norway, Sweden, and Finland are all in Scandinavia.

ⓑ Odin was the father of all gods and men. He was a very wise god.

ⓒ Freya was the goddess of love and beauty. But she was also a warrior goddess.

B

Script

M Teacher: According to Norse mythology, there were a total of nine worlds. These nine worlds existed on three levels. At the top was Asgard, which was the land of the gods and goddesses. In the middle level was Midgard. It meant "Middle Earth." Midgard was the land of humans. There was a rainbow bridge that connected Asgard with Midgard. The name of the bridge was Bifrost. Jotunheim was also on the same level as Midgard. It was the land of the giants. The giants often caused problems for both humans and gods. The third level was the underworld. The best-known place in it was Niflheim. It was a very cold and dark place and was the land of the dead. All of these worlds were connected by Yggdrasil, the world tree. It was an enormous tree that grew from the lowest level to the highest.

1 ⓑ

2 ⓒ

3 ⓐ at top level, land of gods and goddesses

  ⓑ same level as Midgard, land of giants

  ⓒ world tree, connected nine worlds; grew from lowest level to highest

Unit 06 | Creatures in Norse Mythology

Pre-Listening Questions [Sample Answer]

1 The first picture looks like a giant. It's very big. The second picture shows Valkyries.

2 There are giants in Norse mythology. I think there are trolls and dwarves, too.

3 There are goblins called *dokkaebi* and evil spirits called *gwishin*. There are also nine-tailed foxes called *gumiho* in Korean mythology.

Vocabulary

1 fangs

2 claws

3 dragon

Script

M Teacher: There are lots of gods and goddesses in Norse mythology. There are many other creatures, too. Some are monsters, but others aren't.

The Norse gods and goddesses often battled the giants. The giants lived in the land of Jotunheim. But they frequently left Jotunheim to cause problems. The giants had a variety of appearances. Most of them were very large. Some had claws, and others had fangs. But a few of them were actually pleasant to look at.

Many of the monsters in Norse mythology were huge. There was a gigantic wolf named Fenrir. There was also an enormous sea serpent called Jormungand. And Nidhogg was either a giant snake or a dragon. It was always trying to eat part of the world tree Yggdrasil.

Fortunately, not all of the creatures in Norse mythology were monsters. There were elves that lived above the ground and dwarves that lived beneath it. The

Norns were three old women who were very powerful and wise. They were able to influence the destinies of people. Odin had two ravens called Hugin and Munin. They flew around the world every day while watching and listening. Then, they reported everything they saw and heard to Odin.

Finally, there were the Valkyries. These were female spirits that assisted Odin. They watched men fight on the battlefield. When the men died, the Valkyries led the spirits of the bravest and strongest men to Valhalla. This was the hall of the dead for the greatest warriors.

Organizer

ⓐ Giants   ⓑ Lived

ⓒ monsters   ⓓ Elves

ⓔ female   ⓕ Valhalla

Comprehension

1 ⓐ   2 ⓑ   3 ⓐ

4 ⓒ   5 pleasant

6 ⓓ   7 ⓔ   8 ⓐ

9 ⓒ   10 ⓑ

Listening Skills Practice: Note-Taking II

A

ⓐ The giants had a variety of appearances. Most of them were very large. Some had claws, and others had fangs.

ⓑ There was a gigantic wolf named Fenrir. There was also an enormous sea serpent called Jormungand.

ⓒ Finally, there were the Valkyries. These were female spirits that assisted Odin.

B

Script

W Student: For my school report, I researched monsters in Norse mythology. My favorite is Fenrir. Let me tell you about him. He was the son of the god Loki and looked like a giant wolf. The gods were afraid of Fenrir because he was dangerous. So they caught him and locked him in a cage. But Fenrir was very strong, so he escaped. Every time the gods captured Fenrir, he got away. The gods told the dwarves to make a strong chain. The chain was really thin, so it looked harmless. Then, the gods asked Fenrir to put the chain on. Fenrir said he would do that only if one god put his hand in Fenrir's mouth. Tyr agreed to do that. After that, the gods put the chain on Fenrir. He couldn't escape, so, in anger, he bit Tyr's hand off.

1 ⓑ

2 ⓒ

3 ⓐ father of Fenrir

ⓑ made strong chain, very thin

ⓒ put hand in Fenrir's mouth, Fenrir bit hand off

Unit 07

Thor's Wedding

p. 37

Pre-Listening Questions `Sample Answer`

1 I guess Thor is the person sitting down. I don't know the other person.

2 Thor was a Norse god. He liked fighting. He had a big hammer.

3 I suppose he gets married.

Vocabulary

1 veil

2 frost giant

3 hammer

p. 38

Script

W Teacher: One morning, the god Thor woke up. He suddenly realized that his <u>hammer was missing</u>. Thor's hammer was a <u>magic weapon</u> that made him very powerful. He often used it to defeat his enemies in battle. Thor was upset, so he asked Loki <u>for help</u>.

Loki began <u>searching for</u> Thor's hammer. He soon learned that Thrym had stolen it. Thrym was the king of the frost giants. Thrym told Loki he would give back Thor's hammer. But, <u>in return</u>, Freya, the goddess of love and beauty, <u>had to marry</u> him.

Freya <u>refused to marry</u> Thrym, but Loki thought of a clever plan. Loki told Thor to <u>put on</u> a bridal gown. Then, he put a veil over Thor's face. <u>After that</u>, Thor and Loki went to Thrym's palace. Thrym thought Thor was Freya. He was very happy, so he prepared a great feast.

At the feast, the giants were surprised. Thor, who was disguised as Freya, ate a <u>great amount of</u> food. Loki explained that Freya had not eaten for <u>eight days</u>, so she was <u>very hungry</u>. Then, Thrym tried to kiss his bride. He <u>pulled up</u> the veil but saw Thor's red eyes. Loki explained that Freya had <u>not slept for</u> eight nights, so she had red eyes.

Finally, Thrym <u>ordered the giants</u> to give Thor's hammer to Freya. They put the hammer <u>on the table</u>. Thor immediately <u>grabbed the hammer</u> and hit Thrym with it. Then, he killed all of the other giants in the palace, too.

Organizer

ⓐ hammer ⓑ Loki

ⓒ marry ⓓ bridal gown

ⓔ palace ⓕ kills

p. 39

Comprehension

1 ⓒ	2 ⓑ	3 ⓐ
4 ⓒ	5 enemies	
6 ⓑ	7 ⓓ	8 ⓐ
9 ⓔ	10 ⓒ	

p. 40

Listening Skills Practice: Problem and Solution I

A ⓐ S ⓑ S ⓒ P

B

Script

M Teacher: Odin was the wisest of the Norse gods. He was always interested in becoming wiser. But his love of wisdom sometimes caused problems for him. Once, Odin went to Mimir's Well. It was located by the world tree Yggdrasil. Mimir was a creature that guarded the well. The well's waters gave anyone who drank it a lot of knowledge and wisdom. Odin asked Mimir to let him drink from the well, but Mimir refused. Odin asked what he needed to give Mimir to take a drink from the well. Mimir told Odin to give him one of his eyes. Odin thought for a bit. Then, he cut one of his eyes out. Odin dropped the eye in the well and took a drink of water. Odin gained very much knowledge and wisdom, but he lost an eye.

1   ⓒ

2   ⓑ

3   ⓐ ⅲ, S   ⓑ ⅰ, P   ⓒ ⅱ, S

Unit 08   Ragnarok

p. 41

Pre-Listening Questions Sample Answer

1   I can see some gods and monsters in the picture.
2   They are fighting one another.
3   I don't know. I've never heard any end of the world myths.

Vocabulary

1   poison
2   captivity
3   burn

p. 42

Script

M Teacher: Most cultures have stories <u>about the end</u> of the world. In Norse mythology, the name of this event is Ragnarok. It means "fate of the gods." It tells how the gods and their allies fight monsters at <u>a huge battle</u> at the end of the world. <u>Almost all</u> life on the Earth dies during Ragnarok.

First, there will be a time called Fimbulwinter. There will be three years of winter <u>with no summer</u>. Next, the sun and stars will disappear, and the Earth will <u>become dark</u>. Then, Fenrir the wolf will <u>escape from</u> captivity. He will <u>join with</u> Loki, the giants, and many other monsters. They will all travel to Vigrid. They will battle the Norse gods at Vigrid.

The gods will see the armies approaching. They will <u>prepare for battle</u> and go to fight their enemies. According to Norse mythology, the gods <u>already know</u> who they will fight and who will die. For example, Fenrir will kill Odin <u>during the battle</u>. Thor will slay Jormungand the sea serpent <u>with his hammer</u>. But Jormungand's <u>poison will kill</u> Thor. Heimdall and Loki will fight and kill each other.

At the end of the battle, the sky will burn. The Earth will <u>sink underneath</u> the sea. However, that isn't the end of the world. A new Earth will <u>rise above</u> the sea. Some

gods will survive the battle, too. And two humans will survive. They will restart <u>the human race</u>.

Organizer

ⓐ world   ⓑ three
ⓒ die   ⓓ sinks
ⓔ Fenrir   ⓕ prepare

p. 43

Comprehension

1   ⓑ   2   ⓒ   3   ⓐ
4   ⓒ   5   gods

6   ⓑ   7   ⓔ   8   ⓒ
9   ⓐ   10 ⓓ

p. 44

Listening Skills Practice: Problem and Solution II

A   ⓐ P   ⓑ S   ⓒ S
B

Script

W Student: My presentation is about Thor. This is my favorite story about him. One day, Thor visits the giant Hymir. At Hymir's house, Thor eats a lot of food, so Hymir becomes upset. Hymir tells Thor that they have to go fishing together to replace the food Thor ate. The two go out in a boat. Hymir catches a couple of whales, so he's pleased. Then, Thor starts fishing. After a while, something pulls very hard on Thor's line. The sea serpent Jormungand is biting Thor's fishing line. Thor pulls for a long time. He finally gets Jormungand to the surface. Thor grabs his hammer to kill the monster. But Hymir is scared, so he cuts the line. Jormungand manages to escape beneath the ocean. Thor is very angry with Hymir, so he throws the giant into the ocean.

1   ⓑ

2   ⓐ

3   ⓐ ⅰ, S   ⓑ ⅲ, P   ⓒ ⅱ, S

Chapter 3　Famous Discoveries

Unit 09　King Tut's Tomb

p. 47

Pre-Listening Questions　Sample Answer

1　The first picture shows a gold mask. The second picture has a mummy.
2　He was an Egyptian king. He lived a long time ago.
3　The ancient Egyptians made the pyramids and the Sphinx. They made mummies, too. They had lots of different gods and goddesses.

Vocabulary

1　pharaoh
2　mummy
3　ivory

p. 48

Script

M Teacher: In 1341 B.C., Pharaoh Amenhotep IV had a son. He named his son Tutankhamen. Nine years later, Amenhotep had to give up the throne. So, in 1332 B.C., Tutankhamen became the new pharaoh. King Tut was just a boy king. There were no exciting events during his reign. And he was only pharaoh for nine years. In 1323 B.C., when he was around nineteen, King Tut died.

After he died, King Tut's body was turned into a mummy. Then, the Egyptians took him to the Valley of the Kings. They buried many pharaohs and other nobles there. King Tut's mummy and many valuable treasures were sealed in a tomb. Over time, the desert sands buried his tomb. And King Tut disappeared from people's memories.

More than 3,000 years later, Howard Carter was born in 1874. In 1892, at the age of seventeen, Carter made his first trip to Egypt. On that trip, he drew some pictures of Egyptian tombs. He also fell in love with Egypt. So Carter made studying it his goal in life.

In 1917, Carter began excavating areas in the Valley of the Kings. For several years, he found nothing. Then, in November 1922, he discovered a stairway. It led to King Tut's tomb. On November 26, 1922, he opened the tomb. It was mostly in good condition. King Tut's mummy was there. There were jewelry, gold and ivory items, and other valuable objects. Carter's partner asked him, "Can you see anything?" Carter responded, "Yes, wonderful things."

Organizer

ⓐ mummy　　　　　ⓑ pharaoh
ⓒ born　　　　　　ⓓ Egypt
ⓔ tomb　　　　　　ⓕ excavating

p. 49

Comprehension

1　ⓐ	2　ⓑ	3　ⓒ
4　ⓐ	5　wonderful	
6　ⓒ	7　ⓐ	8　ⓑ
9　ⓔ	10　ⓓ	

p. 50

Listening Skills Practice:　Chronological Order I

A　ⓐ 3　　　　ⓑ 1　　　　ⓒ 2

B

Script

M Teacher: People have been building cities for thousands of years. During that time, many cities have fallen. But we mostly know where they're located. Some cities, however, become lost. So people can no longer find them anywhere. For a long time, Petra was one of these lost cities. Petra is located in the modern-day country of Jordan. People started settling in the area of Petra around 1500 B.C. Then, the city itself was built in the second century B.C. Petra was unique because it was built in a valley. There are high mountains on both sides of it. The buildings were also carved into the mountain walls. Petra thrived for many years. But, for some reason, people abandoned it. And no one remembered where it was. People only recalled its name. Then, in 1812, Johann Burckhardt rediscovered Petra. Today, it's known all around the world for the beauty of its ruins.

1　ⓑ

2　ⓐ

3　ⓐ 1500 B.C., 1
　ⓑ 1812, 3
　ⓒ second century B.C., 2

The Rosetta Stone

p. 51

Pre-Listening Questions `Sample Answer`

1 It's a stone from Egypt. It has Egyptian writing on it.
2 I think people learned to read Egyptian writing from the Rosetta Stone.
3 I think it's the name of Egyptian writing. It doesn't use letters. It uses symbols instead.

Vocabulary

1 ruins
2 hieroglyphics
3 text

p. 52

Script

M Teacher: Egypt had one of the greatest civilizations in ancient times. For thousands of years, the Egyptians dominated Northern Africa and parts of the Middle East. The ancient Egyptians left many ruins of their civilization. The Great Pyramid of Giza and the Sphinx were the most famous. There were also ruins, statues, and other artifacts all over Egypt. The Egyptians even had their own language. It was called hieroglyphics. It didn't have letters. Instead, it used pictures and symbols. But there was a problem: No one could read hieroglyphics. For years, people tried to translate various inscriptions. But they didn't succeed.

Then, in 1799, a French army led by Napoleon invaded Egypt. Some French soldiers went to the city of Rosetta. At Rosetta, they discovered a large stone. There was writing in three languages on it. One was hieroglyphics. The other two were ancient Greek and Demotic. The French began studying the stone.

The French didn't keep the stone for long though. In 1801, British forces defeated the French. They seized the Rosetta Stone and took it to England. In 1802, it went on display at the British Museum. Experts realized that they could use the ancient Greek and Demotic inscriptions to understand hieroglyphics. So they studied the Rosetta Stone. It took a long time. But, in 1822, Frenchman Jean Francois Champollion made an announcement. He had translated the text in hieroglyphics. Thanks to him, modern-day scholars know a great deal about ancient Egypt since they can read hieroglyphics.

Organizer

ⓐ East
ⓑ hieroglyphics
ⓒ ruins
ⓓ 1799
ⓔ 1822
ⓕ British

p. 53

Comprehension

1 ⓒ
2 ⓐ
3 ⓑ
4 ⓐ
5 hieroglyphics
6 ⓓ
7 ⓐ
8 ⓑ
9 ⓒ
10 ⓔ

p. 54

Listening Skills Practice: **Chronological Order II**

A ⓐ 3
ⓑ 1
ⓒ 2

B

Script

W News Broadcaster: Here's a report from the world of archaeology. A team of archaeologists in Egypt believes they have found part of the Library of Alexandria. It was once the greatest library in the ancient world. The city of Alexandria was founded in 331 B.C. It soon became one of the most important cities in the Mediterranean region. Its rulers built a great library. Scholars from all over the ancient world went there to learn and study. At one time, the library had around 500,000 books. Its collection included works by Plato, Aristotle, and other great ancient thinkers. But, possibly during the time of Julius Caesar in the first century B.C., the library burned down. Many great books were lost. Later, in the seventh century, much of the city of Alexandria was destroyed. Most people believed the library's location would never be found. But it appears that we now know where it was.

1 ⓒ
2 ⓑ
3 ⓐ seventh century, 3
   ⓑ first century B.C., 2
   ⓒ 331 B.C., 1

Unit 11 Penicillin

p. 55

Pre-Listening Questions Sample Answer

1 He is giving the patient a shot.
2 It can make sick people feel better.
3 Aspirin is a kind of medicine. It is good for headaches.

Vocabulary

1 culture dish
2 mold
3 medical researcher

p. 56

Script

W Teacher: Some of the greatest discoveries in history were accidental. One of the most vital discoveries of the 1900s happened this way. Alexander Fleming made it. He discovered penicillin.

Alexander Fleming was British. He was born in 1881. He was interested in medicine. So he studied to be a doctor. He served as a doctor in World War I. It was a terrible war. Millions of soldiers died. Often, they died because of bacterial infections that they developed after they were wounded.

When the war ended, Fleming became a medical researcher. In 1928, he was studying influenza. One day, he made a great discovery. He had been growing germs in some culture dishes. He noticed that some mold was growing in one of the dishes. Fleming looked carefully at the mold. There was a circle around it that was free of all bacteria. The mold had killed all of the bacteria. Fleming realized the importance of this discovery. So he did more research on it. He named the substance he had found penicilin.

Fleming's discovery was important since bacteria caused many infections. Doctors had no medicines to cure these infections. As a result, large numbers of their patients died. But pencillin was an antibiotic. Therefore it could kill harmful bacteria. Fleming wasn't able to turn penicillin into a medicine though. Two other researchers did that. Since then, doctors all around the world have used penicillin. It has saved the lives of millions of patients.

Organizer

ⓐ doctor ⓑ Served
ⓒ die ⓓ researcher
ⓔ dishes ⓕ mold

p. 57

Comprehension

1 ⓑ 2 ⓐ 3 ⓒ
4 ⓑ 5 antibiotic

6 ⓓ 7 ⓑ 8 ⓔ
9 ⓐ 10 ⓒ

p. 58

Listening Skills Practice: Cause and Effect I

A ⓐ ⓘⓘ ⓑ ⓘⓘⓘ ⓒ ⓘ

B

Script

W Teacher: People with broken bones often get X-rayed. An X-ray shows images of bones inside the body. The discovery of X-rays was an accident. In 1895, German scientist Wilhelm Roentgen was doing experiments in his lab. He took a cathode ray tube. Then, he removed the air from it and filled it with gas. After that, he ran electricity through the tube. He noticed that the tube started to glow. Roentgen realized he had produced a kind of light that no one had ever seen before. He called these rays of light X-rays. He decided to do some experiments with the light. One experiment used his wife's hand. He took an X-ray of it. It showed all of the bones in her hand as well as the ring she was wearing. Many scientists understood that his discovery was important. By 1896, doctors were taking X-rays in hospitals in the United States.

1 ⓐ
2 ⓑ
3 ⓐ Because ⓑ so ⓒ Because

Unit 12 The Microwave Oven

p. 59

Pre-Listening Questions Sample Answer

1 She is using a microwave oven.

2 I'm not really sure. I know it doesn't use heat like regular ovens do.

3 It can cook food quickly. It is pretty cheap, too.

Vocabulary

1 microwave popcorn

2 magnetron

3 radar

p. 60

Script

M Teacher: These days, many homes have microwave ovens. People use microwaves to do various activities. Microwaves can cook food. They can defrost food. They can even make popcorn. And just like some other well-known innovations, the technology that the microwave oven uses was discovered by accident.

In 1946, Dr. Percy Spencer was working at the Raytheon Company. He was doing some work with a magnetron. A magnetron was a device that made microwaves. It was invented during World War II. The military used it for radar.

One day, Dr. Spencer did an experiment with a magnetron. In the middle of the experiment, he became hungry. He remembered that there was a chocolate bar in his pocket. So he reached into his pocket. The chocolate bar was gone though. Instead, there was only melted chocolate.

Dr. Spencer recognized that the magnetron must have melted the chocolate. He became curious. So he did more experiments. He put some unpopped corn in front of the magnetron. Suddenly, the corn started popping. That was the first microwave popcorn. Then, he tried cooking an egg. The egg got hot and blew up in one of his colleagues's faces.

Dr. Spencer and Raytheon believed they could build an oven that cooked food with microwaves. So Raytheon made the first microwave oven. It was big and expensive. So few people used it. Over time, microwaves got smaller and cheaper. Thus more and more people began buying them. Today, they're almost as common as refrigerators are in kitchens.

Organizer

ⓐ scientist   ⓑ magnetrons

ⓒ Chocolate   ⓓ more

ⓔ cook   ⓕ first

p. 61

Comprehension

1	ⓑ	2	ⓑ	3	ⓒ
4	ⓐ	5	Raytheon Company		
6	ⓒ	7	ⓔ	8	ⓐ
9	ⓑ	10	ⓓ		

p. 62

Listening Skills Practice: Cause and Effect II

A   ⓐ ⅱ   ⓑ ⅰ   ⓒ ⅲ

B

Script

W Student: One of my favorite scientists is Sir Isaac Newton. He was one of the smartest people in history. He loved learning. So he studied several fields of science. He did work in optics. He invented calculus. He wrote the three laws of motion. And he also discovered gravity. Many people tell a story about him like this: One day, Newton was sitting underneath an apple tree. Suddenly, an apple fell from the tree and hit him on the head. Because of the apple, he thought about gravity. That's not a true story though. Newton himself said that an apple never hit him on the head. Instead, he was in a garden one night. He saw an apple fall to the ground. Newton wondered why the apple fell down. So he thought about it. And that made him discover gravity.

1 ⓒ

2 ⓑ

3 ⓐ because   ⓑ Because   ⓒ so

Chapter 4   Great Books

Unit 13   *Frankenstein*

p. 65

Pre-Listening Questions   Sample Answer

1 I think he used dead bodies to make the monster.

2 The monster kills lots of people in the book.

3 Vampires are monsters. Werewolves are monsters. Dragons are also monsters.

Vocabulary

1 monster

2 horrified

3 bride

p. 66

Script

W Teacher: The nineteenth century was a great period for literature. Authors wrote many outstanding books then. It was also an age of science. In the 1800s, people made all kinds of scientific discoveries. So science influenced lots of the works that authors wrote.

One of these authors was Mary Shelley. In 1816, she met with a group of authors. One member of the group was her husband, the poet Percy Shelley. Another was the poet Lord Byron. They all decided to try to write the scariest horror story. Sometime later, Mary Shelley had a dream. That gave her an idea for a book.

That book became *Frankenstein*. It was one of the greatest books of her time. *Frankenstein* tells the story of Dr. Victor Frankenstein and the monster he makes. Frankenstein assembles body parts from dead people. Then, he brings his creation to life. Yet he's horrified by the monster.

The rest of the book describes the battle between Frankenstein and the monster. The monster tries to fit in with humans, but everyone rejects him because of his appearance. He becomes angry, so he starts to kill members of Frankenstein's family. He even kills Frankenstein's bride on his wedding night. In the end, Dr. Frankenstein dies. And the monster disappears.

The book *Frankenstein* was a great success. It inspired other writers throughout the 1800s. In the 1900s, the story was told in numerous movies. Today, *Frankenstein* continues to be among the most successful horror stories of all time.

Organizer

ⓐ Mary Shelley ⓑ authors

ⓒ horror ⓓ dream

ⓔ dead people ⓕ horrified

p. 67

Comprehension

1 ⓑ 2 ⓑ 3 ⓐ

4 ⓒ 5 body parts

6 ⓓ 7 ⓒ 8 ⓐ

9 ⓑ 10 ⓔ

p. 68

Listening Skills Practice: Main Idea I

A ⓑ

B

Script

M Teacher: Robert Louis Stevenson was one of the best writers of the nineteenth century. He wrote many different genres of books. One of his most famous novels was *The Strange Case of Dr. Jekyll and Mr. Hyde*. Like many other works written in the 1800s, it focused on science. In the story, Dr. Henry Jekyll is a good man. He likes to experiment in his laboratory. One day, he creates a mixture that turns him into another person. He becomes Mr. Hyde. While Dr. Jekyll is good, Mr. Hyde is bad. In fact, Mr. Hyde is very bad. He commits all kinds of crimes, including murder. *Dr. Jekyll and Mr. Hyde* tells the tale of what happens to both Dr. Jekyll and Mr. Hyde. And it focuses on how people can misuse science when they don't understand it.

1 ⓒ 2 ⓑ 3 ⓒ

Unit 14 *Dracula*

p. 69

Pre-Listening Questions [Sample Answer]

1 Dracula was a vampire. He lived a long time ago.

2 A vampire is a monster. It drinks people's blood.

3 A vampire is very strong and fast. It is much stronger and faster than a human. Sunlight can harm a vampire. So can a cross. Silver can harm a vampire, too.

Vocabulary

1 vampire hunter

2 sunlight

3 stake

Script

M Teacher: There are many <u>monsters in stories</u> that people tell. One of the <u>most frightening</u> ones is the vampire. A vampire appears to be human. But it's actually an undead creature. It survives by <u>drinking the blood</u> of humans. A vampire is usually quite strong. It can also often turn itself into a bat. It has few weaknesses. But sunlight can kill a vampire. Stabbing it <u>in the heart</u> with a wooden stake can kill it. Silver weapons <u>work against it</u>, too.

Irish writer Bram Stoker did research on the <u>many legends</u> about vampires. Then, he wrote the book *Dracula*. He published it in 1897. *Dracula* was a <u>classic horror novel</u> that has influenced numerous other works.

In the story, Count Dracula is <u>a noble from</u> Translyvania. He's also a vampire. Dracula purchases a home in London and makes plans to move there. However, Abraham Van Helsing, a <u>vampire hunter</u>, decovers him. Van Helsing, along with a small group of men, forces Dracula to leave England and to return to Transylvania. Then, they <u>follow the vampire</u> to his home and <u>manage to kill</u> him.

Dracula is one of the <u>best-known</u> monsters these days. But the book *Dracula* wasn't <u>an immediate hit</u>. Instead, it only became <u>popular after movies</u> about it were made. Today, thanks to Bram Stoker's masterpiece, vampire stories are some of the most <u>popular and bestselling</u> works in the world.

Organizer

ⓐ blood   ⓑ sunlight
ⓒ bat   ⓓ Bram Stoker
ⓔ Dracula   ⓕ influenced

Comprehension

1   ⓑ   2   ⓒ   3   ⓐ
4   ⓑ   5   popular

6   ⓔ   7   ⓓ   8   ⓒ
9   ⓐ   10   ⓑ

Listening Skills Practice: Main Idea I

A   ⓒ

B

Script

M Teacher: Here's an interesting story from Poland. We all know that vampires are fictitious monsters, don't we? Or is there some truth to the stories about vampires? Archaeologists recently discovered a gravesite for people believed to be vampires. What they found in the graves was shocking. Apparently, some of the bodies had been given a vampire burial. After the people died, their heads were cut off. Then, their heads were placed on their legs, and they were buried. In the past, people believed that burying people this way would prevent dead people from rising from their graves. Interestingly, there are similar vampire burials in places all around the world. And most cultures around the world have stories about humanlike monsters that drank people's blood. Were there really vampires in the past? I hope not. But it appears that people used to think that vampires really existed.

1   ⓑ   2   ⓐ   3   ⓐ

Unit 15   *Alice's Adventures in Wonderland*

Pre-Listening Questions   Sample Answer

1   Alice is sitting at a table. There are a rabbit, a mouse, and a man with a big hat.
2   It's the title of a book. It's a fantasy story. Alice visits Wonderland and meets some interesting people and animals.
3   *The Lord of the Rings* is a fantasy series. So is *The Chronicles of Narnia*.

Vocabulary

1   Cheshire Cat
2   Mad Hatter
3   caterpillar

Script

W Teacher: One day, a young girl named Alice is sitting with her sister beside a river. She notices <u>a white rabbit</u> with clothes on. The rabbit takes out a watch, looks at it, and exclaims, "Oh, dear. I shall <u>be late</u>." The rabbit then

<u>goes down into</u> a rabbit hole. Curious, Alice follows the rabbit. She soon falls very far into the hole. Then, she winds up in <u>a magical place</u> called Wonderland.

That is <u>the beginning of</u> the book *Alice's Adventures in Wonderland*. Lewis Carroll wrote and published it <u>in 1865</u>. Since it was published, it has become one of the most popular <u>works of fantasy</u> in the world.

While Alice is in Wonderland, she encounters many strange and <u>wonderful creatures</u>. She meets the white rabbit. She also meets a mouse, a caterpillar, and the Cheshire Cat. In the process, she has a number of odd experiences that <u>confuse her</u>. The Cheshire Cat finally explains to her that everyone in Wonderland is mad. Alice has more adventures after that. She even meets the <u>king and queen</u> of Wonderland. Finally, at the end of the book, she <u>wakes up</u> next to her sister. Apparently, she had just been having a dream.

Some of the most <u>colorful characters</u> in literature appear in *Alice's Adventures in Wonderland*. They include the Cheshire Cat, the Mad Hatter, and the <u>Queen of Hearts</u>. The book was <u>so popular</u> that Carroll wrote a sequel: *Through the Looking Glass*.

Organizer

ⓐ Lewis Carroll   ⓑ fantasy
ⓒ rabbit   ⓓ Wonderland
ⓔ strange   ⓕ dream

p. 75

Comprehension

1 ⓐ   2 ⓒ   3 ⓑ
4 ⓑ   5 colorful

6 ⓓ   7 ⓐ   8 ⓑ
9 ⓔ   10 ⓒ

p. 76

Listening Skills Practice: Inference I

A ⓐ ⅱ   ⓑ ⅱ   ⓒ ⅰ
B

Script

M Teacher: George MacDonald lived from 1824 to 1905. He was a Scottish minister, but he also wrote poems and books. Today, few people know about him and his works. But he influenced a large number of writers in the 1800s

and 1900s. MacDonald's most famous work is *The Princess and the Goblin*. Later, he wrote a sequel called *The Princess and Curdie*. He also wrote the fantasy novels *Phantastes* and *At the Back of the North Wind*. He wrote numerous other novels and fairy tales, too. C.S. Lewis, who wrote *The Chronicles of Narnia*, considered MacDonald to be his writing master. MacDonald's works had an influence on J.R.R. Tolkien as well. Tolkien was the author of *The Lord of the Rings* series. Many other fantasy authors have also said that MacDonald's works affected theirs.

1 ⓒ   2 ⓑ   3 ⓑ

Unit 16   *20,000 Leagues under the Sea*

p. 77

Pre-Listening Questions   Sample Answer

1 It looks like a submarine. But the shape is very strange.
2 It's a book about a submarine. It travels all around the Earth.
3 I would love to ride in a submarine. I think it would be fun but a little scary, too.

Vocabulary

1 beast
2 Atlantis
3 submarine

p. 78

Script

M Teacher: Jules Verne was a French author. He lived from 1828 to 1905. Like many other authors from his time, science influenced him <u>a great deal</u>. In fact, people consider him to be the <u>father of science</u> fiction. He <u>wrote famous works</u> such as *Around the World in 80 Days* and *Journey to the Center of the Earth*. These works—and his others—often focused on the science of <u>his time</u> as well as futuristic science.

His novel *20,000 Leagues under the Sea* <u>relies heavily upon</u> science. It tells <u>the tale of</u> Captain Nemo and his submarine the *Nautilus*. Verne published the book in 1869. At that time, there <u>were few submarines</u>. They were all primitive. But Verne's submarine was <u>very advanced</u>. It was like the submarines of today.

The story begins with a tale of a beast _that's attacking ships_. The _Abraham Lincoln_, a ship, sets out to find the beast. It _encounters the beast_, which is really the _Nautilus_. During a battle, three of the _Abraham Lincoln's_ crew members fall _into the ocean_. The _Nautilus_ rescues them.

The rest of the book describes their time _beneath the sea_. The _Nautilus_ _visits places_ that few men have seen. For instance, it goes to Antarctica. It _tours the ruins_ of Atlantis, too.

20,000 Leagues under the Sea is a _thrilling adventure novel_. It uses science and technology that didn't exist in Verne's day. However, Verne _predicted the future_ very well. Many of the advances he describes in the book _exist today_.

Organizer

ⓐ father   ⓑ _80 Days_
ⓒ futuristic   ⓓ submarine
ⓔ Rescues   ⓕ Antarctica

p. 79

Comprehension

1 ⓒ   2 ⓑ   3 ⓐ
4 ⓒ   5 thrilling

6 ⓓ   7 ⓐ   8 ⓑ
9 ⓔ   10 ⓒ

p. 80

Listening Skills Practice: Inference II

A   ⓐ ⅰ   ⓑ ⅱ   ⓒ ⅰ
B

Script

M Student: My favorite writer is Jules Verne. He wrote several books that were based on science. He wrote one book called _Paris in the Twentieth Century_. He actually wrote the book in 1863. But it wasn't published for more than a century. It was published in 1994. Verne put the manuscript in a safe, and no one discovered it for more than a century. I was impressed by _Paris in the Twentieth Century_ because Verne accurately predicted lots of facts about the future in it. For instance, the book features trains that move at high speeds. There are tall skyscrapers made of glass, too. The book also contains several other predictions about the future that came

true. When I read the book, I was amazed by how so many parts of Verne's imaginary world resembled the modern world. That impressed me the most about the book.

1 ⓐ   2 ⓑ   3 ⓑ

Chapter 5   Unique Animals

Unit 17   The Koala

p. 83

Pre-Listening Questions   Sample Answer

1 It lives in Australia.
2 I think it's a mammal.
3 It likes to live in trees. And it's very popular in Australia.

Vocabulary

1 eucalyptus tree
2 fur
3 poisonous

p. 84

Script

W Teacher: Australia has some of the planet's _most unique wildlife_. One animal that people often associate with Australia is the koala. The koala looks _cute and adorable_. Some people even call it a koala bear. But these people are wrong. The koala _isn't a bear_ at all.

The koala is _a small animal_. An adult koala is usually a little more than half a meter _in length_. It might weigh around ten kilograms. It has thick fur. The koala's fur protects it from both _cold and hot_ temperatures. It even keeps the koala dry _when it rains_.

The koala is a marsupial. When a female gives birth, the baby—called a joey—isn't fully developed. In fact, the joey is extremely small. It climbs _into a pouch_ in its mother's body. Then, it _continues to develop_ from inside the pouch. After a while, it _becomes larger_. At that time, it can survive outside its mother's pouch.

The koala spends most of its _life in trees_. It likes the eucalyptus tree in particular. The koala mainly eats the leaves of that tree. This is unique because eucalyptus leaves are poisonous to most other animals. But the koala can eat the leaves without suffering any problems.

Unfortunately, there are fewer and fewer eucalyptus trees in Australia these days. The reason is that people are chopping them down. As a result, there are only around 100,000 koalas in Australia today. And the number of koalas will probably decline even more in the future.

Organizer

ⓐ ten   ⓑ thick
ⓒ babies   ⓓ pouch
ⓔ trees   ⓕ eucalyptus

p. 85

Comprehension

1　ⓐ　　2　ⓑ　　3　ⓒ
4　ⓐ　　5　declining

6　ⓓ　　7　ⓒ　　8　ⓐ
9　ⓔ　　10　ⓑ

p. 86

Listening Skills Practice: **Summarizing I**

A　ⓒ

B

Script

M Teacher: Australia has lots of unusual animals. One's called the duck-billed platypus. It looks like a combination of an otter, a duck, and a beaver. It has the body of an otter. It has the bill and webbed feet of a duck. And it has a tail that looks like a beaver's. It lives on land but prefers the water. So it's a great swimmer. Even though it's a mammal, it lays eggs. This makes it a very odd mammal. Only one other mammal lays eggs like the duck-billed platypus. Another unusual feature is that it can use poison against other animals. But it doesn't have a poisonous bite like a snake. Instead, it has stingers on its back feet. It uses the stingers to inject poison into other animals. All of these characteristics make the duck-billed platypus one of nature's strangest animals.

1　ⓑ　　2　ⓐ　　3　ⓑ

Unit 18   **The Komodo Dragon**

p. 87

Pre-Listening Questions `Sample Answer`

1　It's a lizard.
2　I know it lives on some islands, but I don't know where.
3　It looks like a dragon or a dinosaur.

Vocabulary

1　lizard
2　breathe fire
3　prehistoric animal

p. 88

Script

M Teacher: Dinosaurs once lived all over the planet. They died around sixty-five million years ago though. Today, there aren't any dinosaurs anywhere. There are, however, some creatures that remind people of those prehistoric animals. One of these is the Komodo dragon. It lives on some islands in Indonesia.

The Komodo dragon isn't like a mythical dragon. It doesn't have wings. And it can't breathe fire or speak either. Yet it's still an impressive animal. The Komodo dragon is the world's biggest lizard. It can grow longer than three meters from the tip of its nose to the end of its tail. The average Komodo dragon weighs about seventy kilograms. But the largest one ever caught weighed 166 kilograms.

The Komodo dragon is unusual for a couple of reasons. First, most lizards are omnivores. So they eat both meat and plant matter. The Komodo dragon, on the other hand, is a carnivore. It only eats meat. And, due to its great size, it needs lots of meat. It eats all kinds of small animals. But it also hunts and kills horses, wild pigs, deer, and other animals of similar sizes. It even hunts humans at times.

The lizard bites prey when it attacks. It often doesn't kill its prey with the first bite. But its saliva has many deadly types of bacteria. The bacteria kill any animal the Komodo dragon bites after a few hours. So it simply follows the animal until it dies. Then, it has a meal.

Organizer

ⓐ Indonesia　　　　ⓑ biggest
ⓒ 70　　　　　　　　ⓓ meat
ⓔ Hunts　　　　　　ⓕ Bites

p. 89

Comprehension

1	ⓑ	2	ⓐ	3	ⓒ
4	ⓒ	5	carnivore		
6	ⓑ	7	ⓔ	8	ⓐ
9	ⓓ	10	ⓒ		

p. 90

Listening Skills Practice: Summarizing II

A　ⓐ

B

Script

M Zookeeper: Welcome, everyone, to the newest exhibit at the Springfield Zoo. As you can see, we have created a rainforest ecosystem here. Half of this exhibit has large trees and other vegetation found in rainforests. The other half is a swamp. Thus we have both land and water creatures in this exhibit. Now, look behind me, and you'll see one of our most prized animals. It's the green basilisk lizard. It's an iguana that lives in the rainforest. It's bright green, and it has one or more crests on its back. But that's not why it's so special. Ah, look. There it goes. Take a look at that. The green basilisk lizard is able to run on the water. Isn't that amazing? It can run about 1.5 meters per second on top of the water. Its long toes and extra flaps of skin allow it to do this incredible feat.

| 1 | ⓐ | 2 | ⓑ | 3 | ⓒ |

Unit 19　The Walking Leaf

p. 91

Pre-Listening Questions　Sample Answer

1　I think it's an insect.
2　Yes, I can see it. It is hiding in the leaves.
3　Some lizards and fish use camouflage. And so do tigers.

Vocabulary

1　zebra
2　walking stick
3　camouflage

p. 92

Script

M Teacher: A lot of animals use camoflauge. This means that they hide from other animals. Animals use camouflage in many ways. The easiest way is the color of the animal. Look at many forest animals. Animals like rabbits and deer are often brown. This helps them blend in with the color of the ground. Animals like tigers and zebras have stripes. Their stripes are forms of camouflage as well.

A few animals use camouflage differently. They resemble various inanimate objects. For example, the rockfish resembles a rock. The walking stick looks like a stick from a tree or bush. And the walking leaf resembles the leaf of a tree.

The walking leaf is an insect. It lives mostly in Asia and Australia. It lives in various ecosystems. But it's somewhat common in rainforests. The walking leaf is a fascinating insect because it really looks like a leaf. Sometimes parts of a walking leaf's body even appear to have bite marks on it. That provides even more camouflage for it.

The walking leaf uses its unqiue body to hide from predators. Many animals simply don't notice the walking leaf even if they're next to it. When the walking leaf moves, its body sways from side to side. This makes it appear as if the wind is blowing the leaf. It's a very effective disguise for the insect. And it helps prevent predators from catching and eating it.

Organizer

ⓐ hide　　　　　　ⓑ stripes
ⓒ rock　　　　　　ⓓ leaf
ⓔ rainforests　　　ⓕ wind

p. 93

Comprehension

1	ⓒ	2	ⓑ	3	ⓒ
4	ⓐ	5	camouflage		
6	ⓔ	7	ⓐ	8	ⓓ
9	ⓒ	10	ⓑ		

Listening Skills Practice: Word Stress I

A

ⓐ The (easiest) way is the color of the animal.

ⓑ The walking leaf is a fascinating insect because it (really) looks like a leaf.

ⓒ That provides even (more) camouflage for it.

B

Script

> **W Teacher:** The praying mantis is one of the most unusual-looking insects in the world. Like all insects, it has three body parts. But its front two legs are bent together. They make it appear as if the insect is praying. That's why people call it the praying mantis. This insect is green in color, so it uses camouflage to blend it with grass and other plants. But it does not use camouflage for defensive reasons. The praying mantis is a predator. So it hides in plants to make it easier to attack other animals. It usually hunts other insects. But some praying mantises can grow to very large sizes. They can be more than fifteen centimeters long. As a result, some of them are extraordinary predators. These large animals hunt and kill small reptiles, birds, and even mammals. Now that's impressive.

1 ⓐ

2 ⓒ

3 ⓐ But it does (not) use camouflage for defensive purposes.

　 ⓑ They can be more than (fifteen) centimeters long.

　 ⓒ Now (that's) impressive.

Unit 20 The Hummingbird

Pre-Listening Questions `Sample Answer`

1 I think its eats nectar from flowers.

2 It's tiny.

3 It moves its wings very quickly. And it always flies around going from one flower to another.

Vocabulary

1 helicopter

2 upside down

3 backward

Script

> **M Teacher:** Every spring and summer, there's a common sight in many flower gardens. It's the tiny hummingbird flying from flower to flower. It does this to drink nectar from flowers. Many people who watch the hummingbird notice one unusual thing about it: It does not land but continues to flap its wings as it feeds. However, it doesn't move as it flies. Instead, it hovers like a helicopter.
>
> The hummingbird is unusual for many reasons. First, it's the smallest of all birds. A typical adult hummingbird is around eight centimeters long. It also weighs between only two and twenty grams. But the most unusual feature about this bird concerns how it flies. Like all birds, the hummingbird can fly forward. But, unlike all other birds, the hummingbird can fly backward. It can also fly from side to side to the left or right. It can hover in the air. Finally, it can even fly upside down. No other birds are capable of such aerial feats.
>
> The hummingbird can fly like this thanks to its wings. Its wings can rotate completely in a circle. That lets it fly in so many directions. In addition, the hummingbird flaps its wings very swiftly. While flying, it flaps its wings around eighty times per second. In some instances, it can flap its wings more than 200 times a second. That's incredibly fast. In fact, it's so fast that the bird's wings make a humming sound. That's why it's called the hummingbird.

Organizer

ⓐ smallest　　　　　ⓑ Adult

ⓒ two　　　　　　　ⓓ backward

ⓔ rotate　　　　　　ⓕ 80

Comprehension

1 ⓐ　　　　2 ⓐ　　　　3 ⓒ

4 ⓒ　　　　5 humming

6 ⓓ　　　　7 ⓔ　　　　8 ⓒ

9 ⓐ　　　　10 ⓑ

Listening Skills Practice: Word Stress II

A

ⓐ It does (not) land but continues to flap its wings as it feeds.

ⓑ But, unlike all other birds, the hummingbird can fly (backward).

ⓒ In addition, the hummingbird flaps its wings (very) swiftly.

B

Script

M Teacher: In just a few moments, we're going to enter the cave. We'll explore it for about three hours. I think you're going to have a great time. But you need to know one very important thing: There are bats in these caves. Let me tell you about bats. Now, there's a lot of incorrect information about bats that many people believe. For instance, people often say that bats are blind. I'm sorry, but that's simply wrong. Bats have poor eyesight, but they can still see. When they fly, they rely on something called echolocation. This operates similar to radar. Bats make extremely high-pitched sounds. These bounce off of objects—both living and nonliving ones—and return to the bats. In that way, bats can get images of what is around them. The use of echolocation makes bats very good hunters. And it also makes them really unusual creatures.

1 ⓑ

2 ⓐ

3 ⓐ I think you're going to have a (great) time.

ⓑ Bats have poor eyesight, (but) they can still see.

ⓒ And it also makes them (really) unusual creatures.

Word List

Chapter 1 Astronomy

Unit 01

1 **chunk** *(n)* a large piece of something
A *chunk* of rock broke off when he hit it with a hammer.

2 **completely** *(adv)* entirely; totally
I am *completely* confused by your explanation.

3 **cover** *(v)* to extend over
Clouds *cover* almost the entire sky today.

4 **diameter** *(n)* the width of a circle or sphere
The tree trunk has a *diameter* of one meter.

5 **flash** *(v)* suddenly to become light; to appear suddenly
A light in the house *flashed* several times.

6 **grain** *(n)* a tiny piece of something
There are countless *grains* of sand at the beach.

7 **land** *(v)* to go from the air to the ground
The airplane is supposed to *land* in thirty minutes.

8 **melt** *(v)* to change from a solid to a liquid
Most metals *melt* at very high temperatures.

9 **occasionally** *(adv)* sometimes; from time to time
We *occasionally* visit our grandparents.

10 **solar system** *(n)* the sun and all of the planets and other objects that orbit it
There are eight planets in the *solar system*.

Unit 02

1 **blind** *(adj)* unable to see
The kind boy helped the *blind* woman cross the street.

2 **block** *(v)* to get in the way of
The boxes on the floor are *blocking* the door.

3 **damage** *(v)* to harm
Try not to *damage* anything when you are moving.

4 **dangerous** *(adj)* not safe
Climbing a mountain by yourself can be *dangerous*.

5 **impressive** *(adj)* remarkable; exciting
The team played an *impressive* game and won the championship.

6 **lucky** *(adj)* fortunate; having good luck
You are *lucky* to have such good friends.

7 **partial** *(adj)* incomplete; limited
Some teachers give *partial* credit to students on their exams.

8 **rare** *(adj)* uncommon; unusual
Gold and silver are both *rare* metals.

9 **remind** *(v)* to tell someone about something he or she must do
Please *remind* me about the concert this weekend.

10 **revolve** *(v)* to go around in a circle; to orbit
Jupiter takes several years to *revolve* around the sun once.

Unit 03

1 **bright** *(adj)* giving off a lot of light; brilliant
There are many *bright* lights in the city

2 **collect** *(v)* to gather; to take in
Let's *collect* all of these cans and recycle them.

3 **disagree** *(v)* to think differently than another person; not to agree
I *disagree* with your opinion.

4 **lens** *(n)* a curved substance such as glass that is used to make objects appear to be larger
The telescope has a very powerful *lens*.

5 **mathematician** *(n)* a person who studies or teaches math
John is a *mathematician* and teaches at the local university.

6 **observe** *(v)* to look at; to see
Let's *observe* the animals in the wild for a while.

7 **physicist** *(n)* a scientist who studies physics
The *physicist* made an important discovery about the universe.

8 **telescope** *(n)* a tool used to look at distant objects such as stars and planets
You can see the planets up close with a *telescope*.

9 **theory** *(n)* an idea about something; a hypothesis
Please explain your *theory* one more time.

10 **tutor** *(n)* a private teacher
Janet has a *tutor* come to her house to teach her English.

Unit 04

1 **astronomer** *(n)* a person who studies outer space
The *astronomer* is looking at Venus through her telescope.

2 **canal** *(n)* a manmade waterway connecting two bodies of water
There are many ships in the *canal* right now.

3 **claim** *(v)* to declare; to state
Why are you *claiming* that he stole the money?

4 **couple** *(n)* two; a pair
There are a *couple* of books on the table.

5 **debate** *(n)* a discussion between two or more people; an argument; a disagreement
We will have a *debate* about the topic this evening.

6 **statement** *(n)* a declaration
Everybody believes the *statement* John just made.

7 **topic** *(n)* a subject
The *topic* of the discussion is the planet Mars.

8 **universe** *(n)* the cosmos; everything that exists
No one knows how big the *universe* is.

9 **unknown** *(adj)* unfamiliar; not known; not discovered
There are many *unknown* creatures living on the Earth.

10 **wonder** *(v)* to think about; to consider
Do you ever *wonder* what life in the past was like?

Chapter 2 Norse Mythology

Unit 05

1 **battle** *(v)* to fight
The two armies *battled* each other all day long.

2 **bridge** *(n)* something that connects two pieces of land
The *bridge* goes across the river.

3 **enormous** *(adj)* very large; huge
Many whales are *enormous* animals.

4 **exist** *(v)* to be; to be alive; to live
Do you believe life *exists* on other planets?

5 **giant** *(n)* a very tall monster that often looks like a human
The *giant* stands more than four meters tall.

6   **goddess** (*n*) a female god
Athena and Aphrodite are two Greek *goddesses*.

7   **raven** (*n*) a black bird like a crow
We can see a *raven* sitting on the tree branch.

8   **Scandinavia** (*n*) a part of Northern Europe that includes Denmark, Norway, Sweden, and Finland
It often snows in most parts of *Scandinavia*.

9   **warrior** (*n*) a great fighter; a soldier
The *warrior* challenged all of the others to fight him.

10   **wise** (*adj*) intelligent; clever
Everyone knows that Eric is a very *wise* man.

Unit 06

1   **assist** (*v*) to help
Kevin is going to *assist* Dave with his work.

2   **cage** (*n*) a box that has bars around it
The lion stays in its *cage* because it is so dangerous.

3   **catch** (*v*) to capture; to grab
Let's *catch* some butterflies with the net.

4   **escape** (*v*) to get away from; to get out of
The prisoners tried to *escape* from the police station.

5   **fang** (*n*) the tooth of an animal such as a dog or wolf
That dog has very long *fangs*.

6   **harmless** (*adj*) not dangerous; causing nothing bad to happen
That man is *harmless*, so do not be afraid of him.

7   **pleasant** (*adj*) nice
Yesterday was a very *pleasant* day.

8   **report** (*v*) to write or talk about a topic in depth
Please *report* on what you saw at the factory.

9   **research** (*v*) to study; to investigate
The scientists are going to *research* the moon.

10   **thin** (*adj*) not wide; very small in width
A flower has a very *thin* stem.

Unit 07

1   **clever** (*adj*) smart; intelligent
Clara thought of a *clever* solution to the problem.

2   **explain** (*v*) to talk about something in depth; to describe
Please *explain* the answer to me one more time.

3   **gain** (*v*) to get
I *gained* some information by talking with the teacher.

4   **grab** (*v*) suddenly to take something with one's hands
Karen *grabbed* the pencil from Eric's hand.

5   **immediately** (*adv*) at once; instantly
Contact Mr. Taylor *immediately* if there is a problem.

6   **knowledge** (*n*) information; data
There is a lot of *knowledge* stored on the computer.

7   **missing** (*adj*) gone; lost
The police are searching for the *missing* boy.

8   **refuse** (*v*) to say no to someone; to reject
If you *refuse* to help, we will not finish in time.

9   **steal** (*v*) to take something without paying for it; to rob
Gary tried to *steal* some money, but the police caught him.

10   **well** (*n*) a hole in the ground that has water at the bottom
The farmer is digging a *well* to get water for his farm.

1 approach *(v)* to get close to; to go near
The big dog might bite you if you *approach* it.

2 burn *(v)* to catch on fire
They enjoy *burning* leaves in fall.

3 fate *(n)* destiny; what will happen to a person in the future
The fortuneteller will let you know your *fate*.

4 manage *(v)* to be successful at doing something; to succeed; to accomplish
Steve *managed* to win the game.

5 replace *(v)* to provide a substitute; to change
Let's *replace* the old light bulb with a new one.

6 scared *(adj)* afraid; frightened
Why are you *scared* of the rabbit?

7 serpent *(n)* a snake
We saw a *serpent* in the flower garden.

8 surface *(n)* the upper layer of the water
There are some fish near the *surface* of the lake.

9 underneath *(prep)* below; beneath
You can find the box *underneath* the shelf.

10 visit *(v)* to go to see a person or place
They are going to *visit* their friends after school.

Chapter 3 **Famous Discoveries**

1 abandon *(v)* to leave; to stop living in a place
The people *abandoned* their homes during the war.

2 carve *(v)* to cut into stone, wood, or something hard
The boys *carved* their names into the stone.

3 excavate *(v)* to dig up
We are going to *excavate* the ruins of the ancient city.

4 lost *(adj)* unable to be found
My puppy is *lost*, so I am looking for it.

5 mummy *(n)* the preserved body of a human or animal
The museum has several *mummies* from ancient Egypt.

6 pharaoh *(n)* a king in ancient Egypt
The *pharaohs* ruled Egypt thousands of years ago.

7 rediscover *(v)* to find again
We must *rediscover* the trail since no one remembers where it is.

8 thrive *(v)* to do very well; to prosper
Our company is *thriving* thanks to the good economy.

9 valley *(n)* a low area between two or more mountains
There is a stream running through the *valley*.

10 valuable *(adj)* precious; worth a lot
The pirate buried his *valuable* treasures on an island.

1 ancient *(adj)* very old
This is a gold coin made in *ancient* times.

2 announcement *(n)* a statement; a declaration
The principal will make an *announcement* at nine thirty.

3 **archaeology** *(n)* the study of past civilizations and cultures

Janet wants to study *archaeology* at college.

4 **artifact** *(n)* an object from a long time ago; a relic

We hope to find some *artifacts* when we excavate the ruins.

5 **defeat** *(v)* to beat; to win against

The army *defeated* the enemy in battle.

6 **force** *(n)* an army; a group of soldiers

A large *force* is approaching from the south.

7 **inscription** *(n)* writing on an object such as a statue or stone

Can you read the *inscription* on the statue?

8 **ruler** *(n)* a political leader; a king

Who is the *ruler* of that country?

9 **scholar** *(n)* a person who studies; an academic

Chris is a *scholar* who can read several foreign languages.

10 **text** *(n)* language that is written in a book, magazine, or something similar

I need to translate the *text* on this paper.

Unit 11

1 **accident** *(n)* an unexpected event

Sarah got in a car *accident* in the morning.

2 **decide** *(v)* to choose

We need to *decide* where to go this summer.

3 **discovery** *(n)* the finding of something

Dr. Peters made an important *discovery* in his laboratory.

4 **glow** *(v)* to become light; to shine

A bright light is *glowing* in the park.

5 **serve** *(v)* to work as; to work for

Many men *serve* in the military for a couple of years.

6 **show** *(v)* to exhibit; to display

The picture *shows* how the room used to look.

7 **substance** *(n)* a material

What kind of *substance* is in that container?

8 **terrible** *(adj)* awful; very bad

Peter is sick with a *terrible* cold.

9 **vital** *(adj)* important

It is *vital* for you to remember the instructions.

10 **wound** *(v)* to hurt; to injure

Dave was *wounded* during the battle.

Unit 12

1 **colleague** *(n)* a coworker; a person that one works with

Amy's *colleagues* think she is a hard worker.

2 **device** *(n)* a tool; a piece of equipment

I do not know how to use the new *device* in the office.

3 **expensive** *(adj)* high in price; costing a lot of money

Those clothes are too *expensive* for me.

4 **experiment** *(n)* a test; research

The scientists are conducting an *experiment* this afternoon.

5 **fall** *(v)* to drop to the ground

The boy *fell* to the ground and broke his arm.

6 **garden** *(n)* a small area in which plants are grown

She likes to spend time painting in the *garden*.

7 **gravity** *(n)* the force of attraction; the force that keeps objects from floating off into space

The moon's *gravity* is not as powerful as the Earth's.

8   **optics** *(n)* the study of light
He is planning to study *optics* at his university.

9   **radar** *(n)* a device for detecting the position or movement of distant objects such as aircraft
A submarine was detected by *radar*.

10   **refrigerator** *(n)* a machine that keeps food cold
Put the leftover food in the *refrigerator*, please.

Chapter 4 Great Books

Unit 13

1   **bride** *(n)* a wife; the woman whom a man marries
The *bride* is wearing a white dress at her wedding.

2   **create** *(v)* to make
They are trying to *create* something new.

3   **crime** *(n)* an illegal act; something that is against the law
If you commit a *crime*, you might get in trouble.

4   **genre** *(n)* a kind; a type
Mark's favorite movie *genre* is action.

5   **horrified** *(adj)* shocked; disgusted; upset
They were *horrified* by the news of the bombing.

6   **laboratory** *(n)* a room where a person conducts experiments
There are many different chemicals in his *laboratory*.

7   **misuse** *(v)* to use improperly
Do not *misuse* the machine, or it might break.

8   **mixture** *(n)* a combination of two or more things
Salt is a *mixture* of sodium and chlorine.

9   **novel** *(n)* a fiction book
He wrote a bestselling *novel* in his spare time.

10   **reject** *(v)* to turn down
Mr. Smith *rejected* the proposal Tom made.

Unit 14

1   **appear** *(v)* to seem; to look like
The house *appears* to be in good condition.

2   **bestselling** *(adj)* selling very well; selling better than most others
Thanks to her *bestselling* work, she became a rich woman.

3   **fictitious** *(adj)* not true; false
This story is *fictitious* and is not about real people.

4   **gravesite** *(n)* the place where someone is buried
We visit our grandparents' *gravesite* every year.

5   **humanlike** *(adj)* resembling humans
Some people think that *humanlike* aliens may exist.

6   **immediate** *(adj)* at once; instant
You need to give an *immediate* apology to your teacher.

7   **masterpiece** *(n)* a great work of art
That *masterpiece* is worth millions of dollars.

8   **rise** *(v)* to get up from; to stand up
Tina tried to *rise*, but her legs hurt too badly to stand.

9   **stab** *(v)* to cut with a knife
The two men tried to *stab* each other during the fight.

10   **vampire** *(n)* an undead monster that sucks the blood of humans
Stories about *vampires* are very popular these days.

1 **chronicle** (*n*) a history; a story; a tale
This *chronicle* is about a period of Roman history.

2 **confuse** (*v*) to puzzle; to make someone unable to understand
Paul *confused* us with his explanation on how to solve the problem.

3 **consider** (*v*) to believe; to think
I *consider* this to be the most beautiful painting in the world.

4 **exclaim** (*v*) to state; to declare; to announce
Susan *exclaimed* that she loved her new home.

5 **mad** (*adj*) crazy; insane
He went *mad* after he lost everything in his life.

6 **magical** (*adj*) relating to magic
In the story, the knight carries a *magical* sword.

7 **master** (*n*) a teacher; a person who has a lot of skill at something
Tony is a *master* of painting who teaches many students.

8 **numerous** (*adj*) many; a lot
There are *numerous* ways to get to my house.

9 **sequel** (*n*) the second part of a story
The author is busy writing a *sequel* to his first book.

10 **wonderful** (*adj*) incredible; amazing
We had a *wonderful* time at the Christmas party.

1 **accurately** (*adv*) correctly
You must *accurately* describe what happened to you yesterday.

2 **beast** (*n*) a terrible monster; a dangerous animal
The villagers were all scared of the terrible *beast*.

3 **feature** (*v*) to contain
The movie *features* many action scenes.

4 **manuscript** (*n*) a text; a work written down on paper
The author sent the *manuscript* to the editor.

5 **predict** (*v*) to make a guess about the future
I *predict* that next year will be better than this year.

6 **rescue** (*v*) to save
The man ran into the burning building and *rescued* the baby.

7 **resemble** (*v*) to look like; to seem like
My sister *resembles* a famous movie star.

8 **safe** (*adj*) not dangerous; protected
You will be *safe* if you stay inside during the storm.

9 **skyscraper** (*n*) a very tall building
The biggest *skyscraper* in the city has more than seventy stories.

10 **tour** (*v*) to travel to a place to see the sights
We are planning to *tour* the country on our next vacation.

Chapter 5 Unique Animals

1 **adorable** (*adj*) cute; sweet; lovable
Your new kitten looks so *adorable*.

2 **combination** (*n*) a mixture; two or more things added together
The meal was a *combination* of European and Asian food.

3   **decline** *(v)* to go down
The value of the dollar is *declining* these days.

4   **develop** *(v)* to grow; to get larger
It takes many years for a baby to *develop* into an adult.

5   **fur** *(n)* thick hair that some animals have
The animal's *fur* keeps it warm during the cold winter.

6   **inject** *(v)* to insert; to put a liquid inside something else
The doctor *injected* the medicine into the patient.

7   **prefer** *(v)* to like one more than another
Do you *prefer* to stay home or to go out tonight?

8   **stinger** *(n)* a part of an animal's body that can harm other animals
A bee has a *stinger* that it attacks others with.

9   **unfortunately** *(adv)* sadly
Unfortunately, I do not remember her name.

10   **unusual** *(adj)* different; strange
We thought the colors the painter used were *unusual*.

Unit 18

1   **allow** *(v)* to let; to permit
Her parents will not *allow* her to buy a smartphone.

2   **carnivore** *(n)* an animal that only eats meat
Cats are *carnivores* so do not eat plants.

3   **crest** *(n)* a raised area on the head, neck, or back of an animal
Some dinosaurs had large *crests* of their backs.

4   **ecosystem** *(n)* an environment; a unique outdoor system such as a forest, sea, or plain
There are many different types of *ecosystems* in the country.

5   **exhibit** *(n)* a display; an exhibition
The museum has an *exhibit* on ancient Greece.

6   **feat** *(n)* an act; a deed
The man performed many *feats* that required great strength.

7   **iguana** *(n)* a type of lizard
The *iguana* likes to sit in the sun all day long.

8   **prey** *(n)* an animal that other animals hunt
The lion is looking for some *prey* to catch.

9   **vegetation** *(n)* plants
Many kinds of *vegetation* grow in the jungle.

10   **wild** *(adj)* not tame; uncivilized
The horse is *wild*, so no person has ridden it yet.

Unit 19

1   **bend** *(v)* to curve; to turn
The road *bends* many times on this mountain.

2   **blend** *(v)* to mix; to combine
You must *blend* the ingredients together to make a cake.

3   **camouflage** *(n)* a skill or ability to hide oneself from others
Many animals use *camouflage* to hide from hunters.

4   **differently** *(adv)* in another way
Karen behaves *differently* when she is alone and when she is with her parents.

5   **extraordinary** *(adj)* amazing; incredible
We all believed that the concert was *extraordinary*.

6   **hide** *(v)* to conceal oneself from view; to keep others from seeing oneself
The children are trying to *hide* from the teacher.

7   **predator** *(n)* an animal that hunts other animals
Sharks are some of the most dangerous *predators* in the ocean.

8   **prevent** *(v)* to stop; to keep something from happening
We tried to *prevent* Jim from spending all of his money.

9   **rainforest** *(n)* a jungle; a hot area with many trees and other plants that gets a lot of rain
There are *rainforests* in many countries in South America.

10 **stripe** *(n)* a band; a line
Angela's shirt has red and blue *stripes*.

9   **poor** *(adj)* very bad; awful; terrible
Ann is a *poor* driver, so no one likes to ride with her.

10 **tiny** *(adj)* very small
There are many *tiny* creatures living in the water.

Unit 20

1   **bounce** *(v)* to spring back from something
Joe is *bouncing* the ball off the ground.

2   **cave** *(n)* a large hole in the ground or in a mountain that often has many passageways
We enjoy exploring the *cave* on the weekend.

3   **common** *(adj)* usual; normal; regular
A *common* way to travel is by bus.

4   **eyesight** *(n)* the ability to see
His *eyesight* is getting worse, so he needs glasses.

5   **helicopter** *(n)* a machine that can fly forward, backward, and sideways
Flying in a *helicopter* is an exciting experience.

6   **incorrect** *(adj)* wrong; not right
I am sorry, but your answer is *incorrect*.

7   **nonliving** *(adj)* dead; not alive
Rocks and air are two *nonliving* things.

8   **notice** *(v)* to see; to observe
Did you *notice* how happy Eric looked today?

Memo

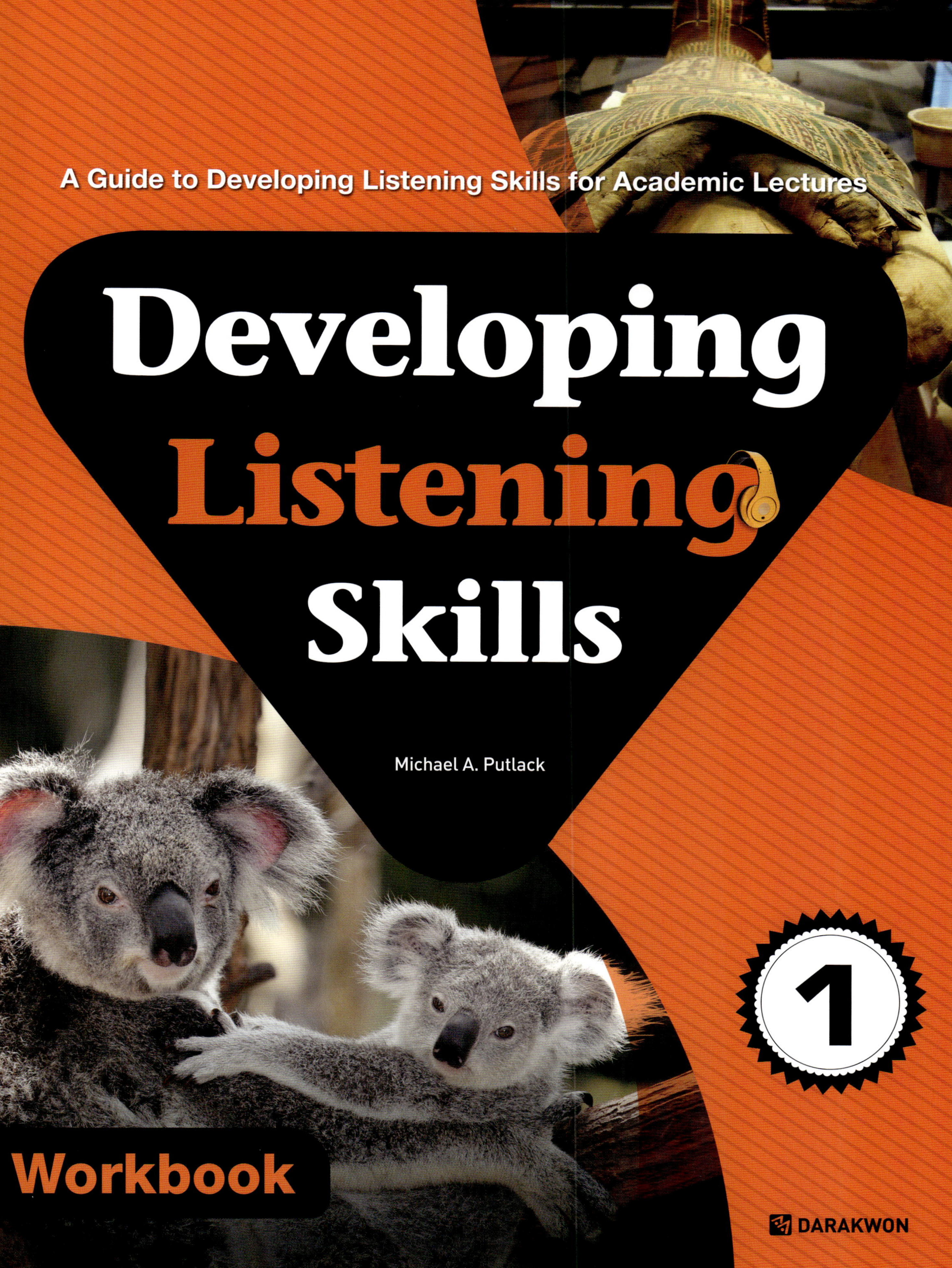

A Guide to Developing Listening Skills for Academic Lectures
Developing Listening Skills
Michael A. Putlack
1
Workbook
DARAKWON

Developing Listening Skills

Workbook

1

DARAKWON

Chapter 1
Astronomy

Asteroids and Comets

A   Listen to the talk on page 12 again. Then, write the answers to the questions.

1   What do moons orbit?

____

2   What are most asteroids made of?

____

3   Where are most asteroids found?

____

4   When do comets get very bright?

____

5   Why do astronomers watch the skies for asteroids and comets?

____

B   Use the words in the box to complete the sentences.

orbit	astronomer	decade	planet	bright

1   There is a __________________ light coming from that room.

2   How long does it take Mercury to __________________ the sun?

3   The __________________ is trying to learn more about the universe.

4   Neptune was the last major __________________ to be discovered.

5   It took Jim nearly a __________________ to save enough money for the trip.

C Listen to the talk on page 14 again. Then, answer T (true) or F (false).

1 ______ A shooting star is really just a meteor.

2 ______ Some meteoroids are also comets.

3 ______ Meteoroids are never as small as grains of sand.

4 ______ A shooting star is burning up in the air.

5 ______ A meteor that lands on the ground is a meteorite.

D Listen to the talk. Then, match the sentences to make comparisons or contrasts.

1 Both of the ideas   ⓐ are interesting ones.

2 Missiles and the solar sail ⓑ requires landing on the asteroid.

3 Only using a solar sail   ⓒ would both change the asteroid's course.

Eclipses

A **Listen to the talk on page 16 again. Then, write the answers to the questions.**

1 What are the two kinds of eclipses?

____

2 What happens when the moon moves between the sun and Earth?

____

3 Which type of eclipse is more common?

____

4 How long can both types of eclipses last?

____

5 What can happen to the moon during a lunar eclipse?

____

B **Use the words in the box to complete the sentences.**

solar	look directly at	constant	lunar	last

1 Do not _________________ the light, or your eyes may be harmed.

2 People in many countries in Asia celebrate _________________ New Year.

3 The game will probably _________________ for about two hours.

4 Some _________________ flares from the sun could harm the Earth if they hit the planet.

5 The two friends keep in _________________ contact with each other.

C Listen to the talk on page 18 again. Then, circle the correct answers.

1   There is going to be a (solar / lunar) eclipse tomorrow.

2   The eclipse will last for around five (minutes / hours).

3   It is going to be a (partial / total) eclipse.

4   The (moon / Earth) will block nearly all of the sun's light.

5   The eclipse could damage people's (ears / eyes).

D Listen to the talk. Then, circle the correct word in each sentence.

1   (Both / Neither) horse and cows return to their barns during a total solar eclipse.

2   Birds go to sleep during a total solar eclipse, (so / but) many insects wake up.

3   Cows become less active during a total solar eclipse, (and / but) lots of birds do, too.

Galileo Galilei

A   **Listen to the talk on page 20 again. Then, write the answers to the questions.**

1   When did Galileo Galilei live?

____

2   For what do most people today remember Galileo?

____

3   What did Galileo make?

____

4   What did Galileo see when he looked at Jupiter?

____

5   What is the name of the model of the universe that Galileo believed in?

____

B   **Use the words in the box to complete the sentences.**

crater	night sky	heliocentric	education	geocentric

1   We enjoy looking at the ___________________ with our telescopes.

2   The belief that everything rotates around the Earth is the ___________________ model.

3   The ___________________ model states that the planets orbit the sun.

4   You can get a good ___________________ by paying attention and studying hard.

5   There is a large ___________________ from an asteroid strike in Arizona, USA.

C Listen to the talk on page 22 again. Then, choose the correct answers.

1 People use _________________ to look at the night sky.

ⓐ telescopes ⓑ eyeglasses ⓒ microscopes

2 Galileo made the first _________________ telescope.

ⓐ radio ⓑ reflecting ⓒ refracting

3 A refracting telescope is good for looking at objects such as _________________.

ⓐ the sun ⓑ the planets ⓒ the stars

4 A reflecting telescope uses _________________ to collect light.

ⓐ lenses ⓑ mirrors ⓒ metal

5 Reflecting telescopes are usually _________________ than reflecting telescopes.

ⓐ bigger ⓑ more expensive ⓒ smaller

D Listen to the talk. Then, complete the outline by filling in the blanks.

Notes

The Hubble Space Telescope

I. Orbits the Earth
  i. Is more than ⓐ _________________ kilometers above the ground

II. Was launched by ⓑ _________________ in 1990

III. Provides very clear images
  i. Telescopes on the ⓒ _________________ don't provide clear images

IV. Is very ⓓ _________________
  i. Has made important discoveries
  ii. Has taken beautiful ⓔ _________________

Percival Lowell

A **Listen to the talk on page 24 again. Then, write the answers to the questions.**

1 What two things do most people remember Percival Lowell for?

____

2 What was the most famous book about Mars in popular culture?

____

3 Why did Percival Lowell think there was life on Mars?

____

4 Which planets did people know about for centuries?

____

5 What did Percival Lowell call the planet he was searching for?

____

B **Use the words in the box to complete the sentences.**

numerous	advance	continue	fascinated	reading public

1 Tim should _________________ to study hard for his test.

2 The scientist made an important _________________ in the field of medicine.

3 Most of the _________________ agrees that Mary's books are well-written.

4 There are _________________ bats living in that cave.

5 I am _________________ by how well John plays basketball.

C **Listen to the talk on page 26 again. Then, fill in the blanks with the correct words.**

1   There is going to be a _________________ at Central Library.

2   Two _________________ are going to talk about Mars.

3   Professor Chapman believes there used to be _________________ on Mars.

4   Professor Perkins thinks there has _________________ been life on Mars.

5   Professor Chapman will give his opening _________________ first.

D **Listen to the talk. Then, complete the outline by filling in the blanks.**

Notes

Life on Mars

I. Have been sending probes to Mars since the 1960s
 i. Study Mars in ⓐ _________________
 ii. Search for ⓑ _________________

II. No evidence of life on Mars

III. Life may have been there in the past
   i. Are robots searching for ⓒ _________________

IV. Will be life on Mars in the ⓓ _________________

   i. Will be humans
   ii. Are plans to send ⓔ _________________ to Mars soon

Chapter 2
Norse Mythology

Norse Gods and Goddesses

A Listen to the talk on page 30 again. Then, write the answers to the questions.

1 Which countries are in Scandinavia?

____

2 What were the names of Odin's ravens?

____

3 What did people often call Thor?

____

4 Who was the Norse goddess of winter?

____

5 Who did the Norse gods and goddesses often fight?

____

B Use the words in the box to complete the sentences.

protect	underworld	is known as	trickster	mythology

1 Larry _________________ the smartest student in our class.

2 A good man always tries to _________________ his family.

3 Stories from Norse _________________ are very entertaining.

4 In some stories, it is possible for a hero to visit the _________________.

5 A _________________ god appears in the stories of many different cultures.

C   **Listen to the talk on page 32 again. Then, answer T (true) or F (false).**

1   _______ There were nine worlds in Norse mythology.

2   _______ Asgard was the land of humans.

3   _______ Midgard means "Middle Earth."

4   _______ The bridge named Bifrost connected Asgard and Jotunheim.

5   _______ Niflheim was the land of the dead.

D   **Listen to the talk. Take notes on the topics written below.**

Notes

1   Yggdrasil: ____

2   Ratatosk: ____

3   the top of Yggdrasil: ____

Creatures in Norse Mythology

A Listen to the talk on page 34 again. Then, write the answers to the questions.

1 Who lived in Jotunheim?

____

2 What was Fenrir?

____

3 Who were the Norns?

____

4 Who were the Valkyries?

____

5 What was Valhalla?

____

B Use the words in the box to complete the sentences.

gigantic	dwarf	sea serpent	battlefield	destiny

1 A _________________ is very short and lives underground.

2 The prince's _________________ is to kill the dragon and to become a great king.

3 The most _________________ animal in the ocean is the blue whale.

4 The two armies are going to meet on the _________________ and fight.

5 In that story, the _________________ lives in the ocean and is ten meters long.

C   **Listen to the talk on page 36 again. Then, circle the correct answers.**

1   Fenrir was the son of (Thor / Loki).

2   The (giants / gods) were very afraid of Fenrir.

3   Fenrir was very (strong / clever), so he always escaped from the cages.

4   One day, the gods asked Fenrir to put on a (thick / thin) chain.

5   Fenrir bit (Loki's / Tyr's) hand off because he was angry.

D   **Listen to the talk. Take notes on the topics written below.**

Notes

1   Sleipner: ____

2   Thor's goats: ____

Thor's Wedding

A Listen to the talk on page 38 again. Then, write the answers to the questions.

1   What magic weapon did Thor have?

____

2   Who looked for Thor's missing weapon?

____

3   What did Thrym want to do?

____

4   What did Thrym see when he pulled up the veil?

____

5   What did Thor do when he got his magic weapon back?

____

B Use the words in the box to complete the sentences.

defeat	order	bridal gown	is disguised as	feast

1   We must _________________ the other team to make it to the final game.

2   Sarah looks beautiful in her _________________.

3   Many Americans have a big _________________ on Thanksgiving Day.

4   The general will _________________ his soldiers to move forward against the enemy.

5   The spy _________________ a harmless old man, but he is actually dangerous.

C Listen to the talk on page 40 again. Then, choose the correct answers.

1 The wisest of the Norse gods was _______________.

ⓐ Thor ⓑ Odin ⓒ Loki

2 Mimer's Well was located by _______________.

ⓐ Yggdrasil ⓑ Bifrost ⓒ Asgard

3 Odin asked Mimir to let him drink from the _______________.

ⓐ lake ⓑ well ⓒ stream

4 Odin had to give Mimir one of his _______________.

ⓐ fingers ⓑ ears ⓒ eyes

5 Odin gained a lot of _______________ after he drank the water.

ⓐ knowledge ⓑ power ⓒ gold

D Listen to the talk. Then, match the sentences to find the problem and the solutions.

Notes

1 The gods called Thor　　　　　ⓐ so they were afraid.

2 Hrungnir threatened the gods,　　　　　ⓑ to challenge the giant.

3 Thor threw his hammer at Hrungnir　　　　　ⓒ and killed the giant.

Ragnarok

A   **Listen to the talk on page 42 again. Then, write the answers to the questions.**

1   What is the battle at the end of the world in Norse mythology?

____

2   What is Fimbulwinter?

____

3   What will happen at Vigrid?

____

4   What will Fenrir do in the battle?

____

5   How many humans will survive the battle?

____

B   **Use the words in the box to complete the sentences.**

battle	restart	disappear	slay	sink

1   You need to _________________ your computer to get it to work properly.

2   They always _________________ when there is a lot of work to do.

3   The ship has a hole in it, so it will _________________ soon.

4   There was a huge _________________ in the valley during the war.

5   The two warriors are trying to _________________ each other in battle.

C   **Listen to the talk on page 44 again. Then, fill in the blanks with the correct words.**

1   One day, Thor visits the ___________________ Hymir.

2   Hymir gets ___________________ because Thor eats all of his food.

3   Hymir catches two ___________________ while they are fishing.

4   The sea serpent ___________________ bites Thor's fishing line.

5   Thor becomes angry, so he ___________________ Hymir into the sea.

D   **Listen to the talk. Then, write P (problem) or S (solution).**

> **Notes**

1   _______ The warriors fought every day to prepare for Ragnarok.

2   _______ The Valkyries brought dead warriors to Valhalla.

3   _______ The gods needed warriors to fight at Ragnarok.

Chapter 3
Famous Discoveries

King Tut's Tomb

A Listen to the talk on page 48 again. Then, write the answers to the questions.

1 How long was King Tut the king of Egypt?

____

2 Why did people forget about King Tut?

____

3 What did Howard Carter do on his first trip to Egypt?

____

4 When did Howard Carter discover King Tut's tomb?

____

5 What did Howard Carter say when his partner asked, "Can you see anything?"

____

B Use the words in the box to complete the sentences.

reign	tomb	fall in love with	bury	excavate

1 The dog is going to ___________________ the bone in the backyard.

2 We will try to ___________________ the ruins in the morning.

3 How long did she ___________________ as the queen of the country?

4 I think that he is going to ___________________ that woman.

5 The king's ___________________ is located near the palace.

C **Listen to the talk on page 50 again. Then, answer T (true) or F (false).**

1 _______ Petra was a lost city for a long time.

2 _______ People began to live in Petra around 1500 A.D.

3 _______ There are high mountains around Petra.

4 _______ Petra was destroyed during a war.

5 _______ Johann Burckhardt rediscovered Petra in the 1800s.

D **Listen to the talk. Then, put the sentences in chronological order.**

Notes

1 _______ A person found some ruins in Crete.

2 _______ A great civilization in Knossos, Crete, existed.

3 _______ Arthur Evans discovered an enormous palace.

The Rosetta Stone

A   Listen to the talk on page 52 again. Then, write the answers to the questions.

1   Which regions did the ancient Egyptians dominate?

____

2   What was hieroglyphics?

____

3   Which three languages were on the Rosetta Stone?

____

4   Where did the British display the Rosetta Stone?

____

5   Who translated the hieroglyphics on the Rosetta Stone?

____

B   Use the words in the box to complete the sentences.

go on display	inscription	translate	seize	dominated

1   The mummies will _________________ in the largest room in the museum.

2   The government plans to _________________ the possessions of some citizens.

3   Can you read the _________________ on the tablet?

4   England _________________ much of the world for a couple of centuries.

5   It takes many years to be able to _________________ a foreign language well.

C   **Listen to the talk on page 54 again. Then, circle the correct answers.**

1   The Library of Alexandria was the (greatest / nicest) library in the ancient world.

2   Alexandria was one of the most important cities in the (Atlantic / Mediterranean) region.

3   There were more than (500,000 / 5,000,000) books in the library at one time.

4   The library may have (burned down / improved) during the time of Julius Caesar.

5   Much of (Egypt / Alexandria) was destroyed in the seventh century.

D   **Listen to the talk. Then, write the correct times in the blanks in the sentences and put them in chronological order.** 

1   _______   The Romans and Jews fought during _________________.

2   _______   Jews wrote the Dead Sea Scrolls _________________ ago.

3   _______   In _________________, some shepherds found the Dead Sea Scrolls.

Penicillin

A **Listen to the talk on page 56 again. Then, write the answers to the questions.**

1 What did Alexander Fleming do during World War I?

____

2 What did Alexander Fleming do after World War I ended?

____

3 What was special about the mold Alexander Fleming was growing?

____

4 What is penicillin?

____

5 How has penicillin helped people?

____

B **Use the words in the box to complete the sentences.**

bacterial infection	accidental	influenza	antibiotic	germs

1 Wash your hands so that you can kill all of the _________________ on them.

2 The doctor thinks that the patient has a _________________.

3 Many people die from _________________ every year.

4 It was an _________________ mistake that I did not mean to do.

5 You should take this _________________ for the next week.

C **Listen to the talk on page 58 again. Then, choose the correct answers.**

1 X-rays can show images of _________________ inside a body.

ⓐ muscles   ⓑ cells   ⓒ bones

2 William Roentgen filled a cathode ray tube with _________________.

ⓐ liquid   ⓑ metal   ⓒ gas

3 The electricity made the tube produce a new kind of _________________.

ⓐ light   ⓑ sound   ⓒ smell

4 William Roentgen took an X-ray of his wife's _________________.

ⓐ head   ⓑ hand   ⓒ foot

5 Doctors in _________________ began using X-rays in 1896.

ⓐ the United States   ⓑ England   ⓒ Germany

D **Listen to the talk. Then, write C (cause) or E (effect) for each sentence.**

Notes

1 _______ James Lind discovered that eating fruit could prevent scurvy.

2 _______ People tried to find a cure for scurvy.

3 _______ Scurvy caused many sailors to get sick on long sea voyages.

The Microwave Oven

A Listen to the talk on page 60 again. Then, write the answers to the questions.

1 What can microwaves do?

____

2 What machine was Dr. Percy Spencer doing work with?

____

3 What melted in Dr. Percy Spencer's pocket?

____

4 What did the egg that Dr. Percy Spencer experimented with do?

____

5 What was the first microwave oven like?

____

B Use the words in the box to complete the sentences.

defrost	innovation	in the middle of	blow up	melt

1 John is _________________ doing an experiment right now.

2 Please _________________ this frozen meat so that we can eat dinner tonight.

3 Be careful, or else the bomb is going to _________________.

4 Ice begins to _________________ above zero degrees Celsius.

5 One great _________________ was the invention of the telephone.

C **Listen to the talk on page 62 again. Then, fill in the blanks with the correct words.**

1 Sir Isaac Newton was one of the __________________ people in history.

2 Sir Isaac Newton wrote the __________________ laws of motion.

3 Sir Isaac Newton discovered ________________.

4 Some people say that an __________________ hit Sir Isaac Newton on the head.

5 Sir Isaac Newton said that he saw a fruit __________________ to the ground in a garden.

D **Listen to the talk. Then, write C (cause) or E (effect) for each sentence.**

Notes

1 ______ Alfred Nobel's brother died in an explosion.

2 ______ Alfred Nobel became a very rich man.

3 ______ Alfred Nobel tried to make a stable explosive.

Chapter 4
Great Books

Frankenstein

A **Listen to the talk on page 66 again. Then, write the answers to the questions.**

1 What influenced a lot of authors in the 1800s?

____

2 What kind of work did Mary Shelley's group members decide to write?

____

3 What does Dr. Frankenstein do?

____

4 How does Dr. Frankenstein feel about his creation?

____

5 What happens at the end of the book?

____

B **Use the words in the box to complete the sentences.**

assemble	literature	horror story	fit in with	battle

1 The two sides will __________________ each other to determine the winner.

2 What is the scariest __________________ you have ever read?

3 There are many great works of __________________ that we need to read.

4 Some people do not __________________ others very well.

5 I will try to __________________ the parts, but putting it together will be hard.

C **Listen to the talk on page 68 again. Then, answer T (true) or F (false).**

1 _______ Robert Louis Stevenson wrote in the eighteenth century.

2 _______ *The Strange Case of Dr. Jekyll and Mr. Hyde* focused on magic.

3 _______ Dr. Jekyll is a good man.

4 _______ Dr. Hyde commits many crimes.

5 _______ *The Strange Case of Dr. Jekyll and Mr. Hyde* points out how people can misuse science.

D **Listen to the talk. Then, choose the main idea.**

ⓐ *Jurassic Park* is about the dangers of people misusing science.

ⓑ The man invites several people to spend a few days on the island with the dinosaurs.

ⓒ The dinosaurs escape, and they kill many people.

Unit 14 — Dracula

A   **Listen to the talk on page 70 again. Then, write the answers to the questions.**

1   How do vampires survive?

____

2   What can vampires turn into?

____

3   Who wrote *Dracula*?

____

4   Where is Count Dracula from?

____

5   When did *Dracula* become popular?

____

B   **Use the words in the box to complete the sentences.**

undead creature	purchase	noble	frightening	weakness

1   A zombie is an _________________, and so are mummies and skeletons.

2   He is a _________________ and comes from a rich family in Europe.

3   In the book, the dragon is very powerful, but it has one _________________.

4   Would you please _________________ two concert tickets for me?

5   The scene in the movie was so _________________ that some people screamed.

C **Listen to the talk on page 72 again. Then, circle the correct answers.**

1   Archaeologists found a (church / gravesite) for people believed to be vampires.

2   In a vampire burial, a person's (head / foot) is cut off.

3   People used vampire burials to prevent the dead from (rising from / spinning in) their graves.

4   There were vampire burials (in a few places / all around the world).

5   In the past, people (believed / didn't believe) in vampires.

D **Listen to the talk. Then, choose the main idea.**

ⓐ There are also stories about humans that can change into other types of animals.

ⓑ A werewolf is a monster that looks like a human but can turn into a wolf.

ⓒ When a werewolf bit a person, that person also turned into a monster.

Alice's Adventures in Wonderland

A Listen to the talk on page 74 again. Then, write the answers to the questions.

1 What animal does Alice see before she falls down the hole?

____

2 Who wrote *Alice's Adventures in Wonderland*?

____

3 What does the Cheshire Cat tell Alice?

____

4 What happens at the end of *Alice's Adventures in Wonderland*?

____

5 What is *Through the Looking Glass*?

____

B Use the words in the box to complete the sentences.

wind up	encounter	odd	looking glass	colorful character

1 The Mad Hatter is a very __________________ in *Alice's Adventures in Wonderland*.

2 I think it is ________________ that Joe does not want to eat lunch with us.

3 If you go straight for five minutes, you will _________________ at the big park.

4 The knight wants to ________________ the dragon so that he can fight it.

5 You can look at your image with that _________________ over there.

C **Listen to the talk on page 76 again. Then, choose the correct answers.**

1 George MacDonald wrote _________________ and books.

ⓐ myths ⓑ songs ⓒ poems

2 George MacDonald _________________ many writers in the 1800s and 1900s.

ⓐ influenced ⓑ taught ⓒ met

3 George MacDonald's most famous work is _________________ .

ⓐ *Phantastes* ⓑ *The Princess and Curdie* ⓒ *The Princess and the Goblin*

4 _________________ considered George MacDonald to be his writing master.

ⓐ C.S. Lewis ⓑ J.R.R. Tolkien ⓒ Lewis Carroll

5 Many _________________ writers said that George MacDonald's works were important to them.

ⓐ poetry ⓑ fantasy ⓒ nonfiction

D **Listen to the talk. Then, answer the question.**

Notes

What can be inferred about the animals in *The Wind in the Willows*?

ⓐ They prefer Toad Hall to the forest.

ⓑ They get along well with humans.

ⓒ They sometimes act like humans.

20,000 Leagues under the Sea

A Listen to the talk on page 78 again. Then, write the answers to the questions.

1 What influenced Jules Verne's writing?

____

2 What is the *Nautilus*?

____

3 What ship tries to find the beast attacking other ships?

____

4 Where does the *Nautilus* visit?

____

5 What kind of novel is *20,000 Leagues under the Sea*?

____

B Use the words in the box to complete the sentences.

a great deal	set out	primitive	thrilling	futuristic

1 We will _______________ on our journey tomorrow morning.

2 This is a _______________ novel about life 100 years from now.

3 That rich man donates _______________ of money to charity.

4 The football game was so _______________ because both teams played well.

5 Some _______________ tribes of people still live in the Amazon Rainforest.

C Listen to the talk on page 80 again. Then, fill in the blanks with the correct words.

1 Jules Verne wrote the book *Paris in the* _______________ *Century.*

2 The book was published about _______________ years after Jules Verne wrote it.

3 Jules Verne correctly _______________ the future in the book.

4 Jules Verne wrote about tall _______________ made of glass.

5 The writer was _______________ with Jules Verne's predictions about the future.

D Listen to the talk. Then, answer the question.

What can be inferred about Phileas Fogg?

ⓐ He was single when he started his journey.

ⓑ He was best friends with Passepartout.

ⓒ He enjoyed making bets with many people.

Chapter 5

Unique Animals

The Koala

A Listen to the talk on page 84 again. Then, write the answers to the questions.

1 What do many people call the koala?

____

2 What kind of animal is a koala?

____

3 What is a joey?

____

4 Why is it unique that the koala eats the leaves of the eucalyptus tree?

____

5 About how many koalas are there in Australia today?

____

B Use the words in the box to complete the sentences.

extremely	marsupials	pouch	chop down	suffer

1 Many ____________________, such as the koala, live in Australia.

2 The woodsman is going to __________________ that large tree in the forest.

3 Can you turn on the heater? It is __________________ cold in this house.

4 You will __________________ many problems if you make the wrong choices in life.

5 The baby koala climbed into its mother's __________________.

C **Listen to the talk on page 86 again. Then, answer T (true) or F (false).**

1 _______ The duck-billed platypus lives in New Zealand.

2 _______ The duck-billed platypus has the body of a beaver.

3 _______ The duck-billed platypus is a mammal.

4 _______ The duck-billed platypus has a poisonous bite.

5 _______ The duck-billed platypus is one of nature's strangest animals.

D **Listen to the talk. Then, choose the correct summary sentence.**

ⓐ Some kangaroos can jump more than ten meters.

ⓑ The kangaroo is an Australian marsupial that can hop and jump.

ⓒ A baby kangaroo lives in its mother's pouch for a while.

The Komodo Dragon

A   **Listen to the talk on page 88 again. Then, write the answers to the questions.**

1   Where does the Komodo dragon live?

____

2   How long can the Komodo dragon grow?

____

3   What does the Komodo dragon eat?

____

4   What does the Komodo dragon hunt?

____

5   What is in the saliva of the Komodo dragon?

____

B   **Use the words in the box to complete the sentences.**

creature	mythical	saliva	impressive	omnivore

1   You create ___________________ in your mouth.

2   Alice's work in the class was very ___________________.

3   I do not know what kind of ___________________ that animal is.

4   An ___________________ eats both meat and vegetation.

5   One of the best-known ___________________ monsters is the dragon.

C   **Listen to the talk on page 90 again. Then, circle the correct answers.**

1   The zoo has created a (riverside / rainforest) ecosystem.

2   The green basilisk lizard is a(n) (iguana / chameleon).

3   The green basilisk lizard is (dark / bright) green in color.

4   It is possible for the green basilisk lizard to (run on / swim under) water.

5   The green basilisk lizard has (long / short) toes.

D   **Listen to the talk. Then, choose the correct summary sentence.**

ⓐ All animals have different life spans.

ⓑ Tortoises live very long lives.

ⓒ Some insects live for a few days.

The Walking Leaf

A   Listen to the talk on page 92 again. Then, write the answers to the questions.

1   Why do animals use camouflage?

____

2   Why are rabbits and deer often brown?

____

3   What does the walking leaf resemble?

____

4   Where does the walking leaf mostly live?

____

5   What happens when the walking leaf moves?

____

B   Use the words in the box to complete the sentences.

fascinating	disguise	sway	resembles	inanimate object

1   Many people say that Tom _________________ a famous movie star.

2   You should wear a _________________ so that no one will know who you are.

3   A rock is an _________________ because it is not alive.

4   The leaves of the tree _________________ back and forth when the wind blows.

5   I think it is _________________ that the walking stick looks like a real stick.

C **Listen to the talk on page 94 again. Then, choose the correct answers.**

1 The praying mantis has __________________ body parts.

   ⓐ two   ⓑ three   ⓒ four

2 The __________________ two legs of the praying mantis are bent together.

   ⓐ front   ⓑ middle   ⓒ back

3 The praying mantis is __________________ in color.

   ⓐ red   ⓑ green   ⓒ black

4 The praying mantis usually hunts __________________.

   ⓐ birds   ⓑ small mammals   ⓒ insects

5 Some praying mantises can grow to be more than __________________ centimeters long.

   ⓐ fifteen   ⓑ twenty   ⓒ thirty

D **Listen to the talk. Then, circle the words that the speaker stresses.**

Notes

1 Sometimes a swarm of cicadas can make very loud sounds.

2 The reason is that there can be more than one million cicadas in a single swarm.

3 Some cicadas spend years living underground.

The Hummingbird

A Listen to the talk on page 96 again. Then, write the answers to the questions.

1 What does the hummingbird drink from flowers?

____

2 What does the hummingbird resemble while it feeds?

____

3 How small is a typical hummingbird?

____

4 In which directions can the hummingbird fly?

____

5 How fast can the hummingbird flap its wing?

____

B Use the words in the box to complete the sentences.

nectar	flap its wings	aerial feat	rotate	hover

1 The butterfly is drinking some __________________ from the flower.

2 You must __________________ the handle to get the door to open.

3 A helicopter can __________________ in the air and stay in the same place.

4 This bird can __________________ several times a second and fly quickly.

5 The pilot will do an __________________ in his plane to impress the people watching.

C **Listen to the talk on page 98 again. Then, fill in the blanks with the correct words.**

1   There are many bats living in the _________________.

2   Many people think that bats are _________________.

3   Bats use _________________ when they fly.

4   Bats make very high-pitched _________________ when they fly.

5   Bats are excellent _________________ because they use echolocation.

D **Listen to the talk. Then, circle the words that the speaker stresses.**

1   However, it does something extremely unusual.

2   Then, the male hornbill builds a wall of mud to close the hole.

3   She stays in the nest until after the eggs hatch.

memo

memo

memo

Developing Listening Skills Book 1

Developing Listening Skills Book 1 has several objectives. First, it will help learners improve their English abilities, particularly their listening skills. Next, it will teach them valuable knowledge about a wide range of academic topics. The talks themselves will also entertain learners as they listen to them. Finally, *Developing Listening Skills Book 1* will help learners prepare for various standardized tests that they may take in the future. For instance, many questions about the talks are similar to those that appear on the iBT TOEFL® Junior and iBT TOEFL® exams. So, by using this book, learners should be able to get higher scores on the tests they take in the future.

For Basic-Level Listeners

Developing Listening Skills Book 1
Developing Listening Skills Book 2

For Intermediate-Level Listeners

Mastering Listening Skills Book 1
Mastering Listening Skills Book 2

Special Features

- **Academic and Entertaining Listening Talks**
  Contains 20 listening talks on all kinds of academic subjects

- **Listening Comprehension and Vocabulary Review Questions**
  Lets listeners test their comprehension of the talks

- **Useful Listening Skills**
  Teaches listeners important skills to make them better at listening

- **Detailed Word List**
  Provides definitions and sample sentences of difficult vocabulary words

- **Comprehensive Workbook**
  Contains extra questions, vocabulary exercises, and listening skill exercises

- **Recordings of Listening Talks**
  Lets listeners improve their listening and pronunciation skills by listening to native speakers